29 Angel

*The Story of a Victorian Terrace in 1930s London
and the People Who Lived There*

29 Angel

The Story of a Victorian Terrace in 1930s London and the People Who Lived There

Stanley Gordon Tinsley

Collated, edited, introduced and appended
by his daughter,

Barbara Tinsley

First Printing: 2019

ISBN 978-0-244-80381-0

Published by Barbara Tinsley

Distributed by Lulu.com

Contents

Introduction

Dispossessed!

by Barbara Tinsley

29 Angel Walk, Hammersmith, the house in which my father was born in 1923 and where I lived with my parents from 1947 to 1964, was demolished in the mid-1960s to make way for a car park for the staff who worked in the towering office block recently built on the large patch of waste ground behind our street.

This waste ground, which may once have been the garden of a large derelict house, was my earthly paradise. Surrounded by a tall metal fence, but accessible from our garden by climbing over our garden wall, it was a secret playground for me, containing trees, buddleia bushes, rose bay willow, goldenrod, Michaelmas daisies, and a large rambling blackberry bush. I was fortunate to spend my childhood in this urban Eden before it was all swept away as part of the spate of property development which took place in 1960s London. With a little foresight and careful planning, the street could have been saved, but instead was sold by our private landlord to property developers. Long before the gentrification of such houses came about, the street was lived in by ordinary working people. At today's prices, and with period housing at a premium, had it been modernised, it would now be worth at least a million. That is the price of houses in a similar, but much meaner, street in Hammersmith today. When my father was a boy, this particular nearby street, which shall remain anonymous, was lived in by the lowest paid workers, many of whom were notorious for their rowdy behaviour. If my grandfather had been told that such houses would be worth a million today, he would have said, "Get out of it!" and laughed us to scorn. The rent for a one bedroomed flat in the house opposite our vanished terrace is £300 a week today. In the 1930s, the rent for our house was eight shillings a week. Our house was certainly built before 1893, as that was the year my grandmother was born, and she had lived in it with her mother and father, three younger sisters and a brother.

We were the first family to leave when notice to quit the street was given. My father, working for the Post Office Savings Bank in Acton, had been offered promotion at the new headquarters in Milburngate in Durham. It seemed an ideal opportunity at the time. After all, where would we have been rehoused? Probably in some high-rise block of flats. Perhaps it was all for the best.

When my father locked the door for the last time and we walked down the doomed street to catch the train to Durham, little did I realise the quality of what we were leaving behind. Shortly before, my father had defiantly painted our panelled front door a bright daffodil yellow with black panels. The old house would look its best before its sad demise. The word 'Letters' was embossed on our letterbox in flowing script. A weigela bush bloomed in the small front garden, which was surrounded by a privet hedge. The sash windows were wide and spacious with wooden shutters inside. It had ceiling bosses, brass light switches, two good sized bedrooms with original iron fireplaces, and a small bedroom at the back. It also had no bathroom. Instead, it had an outside W.C. and one cold tap in the kitchen. The rent then, in 1964, was well under £20 a week.

When we left Angel Walk to move to Durham, my father did not talk about the house we had left behind. He had a new job to look forward to, as a higher clerical officer, and at first seemed optimistic about the new challenge. Disillusion still set in, however. In a supervisory capacity, he did not enjoy the work as much as he had as an ordinary clerical officer, and boredom caused him to become depressed. Highly literate, and an avid reader, he began to write short stories for the *London Evening Standard*, many of which were published. He would spend most evenings clacking away on an old typewriter bought for the purpose.

After his death in 1998, as I was sorting through some of the rough drafts of his short stories, I came across a brown cardboard folder on which was written '29 Angel'. On looking inside, I found it contained a manuscript all about life in our old house. He had kept this project secret from my mother and me, but it probably helped to alleviate the nostalgia which he felt for his lost childhood home. When I read it, I was fascinated by both the affluence and the inconvenience of life in those days: the abundance of food, toys and books, but the total absence of the modern facilities or labour-saving devices we have today.

This is the story of that house and the people who lived there. My father's original manuscript begins here, so now I will let him speak for himself...

29 Angel

*The Story of a Victorian Terrace in 1930s London
and the People Who Lived There*

Stanley Gordon Tinsley

Chapter 1

Sid and Nance

There was never another house like 29 Angel, the house where I was born in 1923.

The first thing you noticed was the panelled front door, imaginatively painted by my father, one year in bright daffodil yellow with black panels, black with yellow panels the next, maroon and blue, coffee and cream, and all kinds of colour combinations over the years. On the glass fanlight above, my father, a sign-writer for London Transport, had scrolled '29' in black, edged with gold. He did not want any letters going astray and ending up in the hands of 'those buggers next door'. My dad had no time for neighbours, nice or otherwise. If he spotted one curtain-peeping while he was painting the door, over he'd stride to squat before the window, scratching at his armpits and leering like some demented ape. Then he would return and wipe off the paint with a rag and turps before putting on a totally new colour, all done to perplex and intrigue the neighbours.

"You shouldn't have done that, Sid," my mum would say in her affectedly refined kind of way. "Squatting down like that in front of people's windows… Whatever will they think?"

"What I want them to think, my girl: that we're anti-social. And by God that's how I want it to be!" He always addressed mum as 'girl' or 'my girl' or 'Nance', his nickname for Ann, her real name.

My dad, taciturn and grumpy with a shaggy head of grey and black hair, bore a remarkable resemblance to Lloyd George. He wanted mum all to himself, and resented any kind of social interaction with friends, neighbours or relatives.

My dad was like that: a man of his time, a chauvinist. He went out and grafted, and, in his opinion, a woman's place was in the home. In those days most of the women in our street were encased in the ubiquitous flowered pinny, the uniform of the stay-at-home wife.

In front of the striking front door was the garden, a small patch of earth graced by a flourishing weigela shrub, its pink, white tipped flowers dancing delicately in the slightest breeze. They seemed to say, "Look! Here beneath our blushing skirts, someone has planted tiger-faced pansies and one or two pompom flowers! The people who live here can't be that bad if they like flowers." That is what my mother thought. She had planted the flowers, and often knelt in the garden to dig out weeds, revealing the well-muscled calves formed in her dancing days.

Born in 1893, she had known an Edwardian girlhood and had met my dad at a dance. Dancing was something they did have in common. In his youth, my dad had essayed to appear on stage as an eccentric dancer in the style of Max Wall, at smoking concerts, old people's teas, private parties and such. I believe that is the one thing mum admired about him.

The question came up often and was never answered: was Angel Road, later renamed Angel Walk, named after the pub at the top of the street, or was the pub named after the road? The only conclusion reached in sporadic debate was this: there were no bleedin' angels living in Angel Road.

29 Angel had scrolled, spearpoint railings all along the width of the front garden to the squeaky front gate. Our railings had to be different from anyone else's, of course. My father didn't and wouldn't paint them, ever. He said that the heavy iron would not rust through in his lifetime, and he did not want passing burglars to get the idea that he had money to waste on weatherproof paint. One of the railings was loose in both its top and bottom rail holes. When I was in a temper with any kid in the street, out came that railing to terrify. Two hands it took to lift it, but I could still find breath to yell like a warrior behind that shield, and a threatened young body didn't half back away sharpish.

The front gate screeched like a banshee. Why the old man wouldn't oil it was probably due to a streak of perversity. Mum told him about it often enough. "Its screech is a constant irritation to a person of my sensitivity," she would say. She spoke like this, my mum. She was better class. At least she thought so. After all, her father had owned his own business as a butcher, and had actually employed a young apprentice. This was something she often mentioned.

Flagstones ran up to the thick, panelled front door. These flagstones, deep and firmly embedded, glistened like washed toffee after rain, and when they dried I could scratch my name on them:

'Stanley Tinsley, born 1923, in Hammersmith, London, England, Europe, Earth, the World, the Universe, not dead yet'.

How distinctive our privet hedge was from that of number 27! Ours burgeoned a lovely lemon yellow, a tightly clustered barrier ensuring a little privacy for a small boy crouched when playing hide and seek, or there for a more clandestine reason. I loved to listen in on conversations of passers-by. Sometimes a woman stopped to straighten up a sagging stocking, and there stretched the shining spectacle of sheathed thigh all the way up. A glimpse of knicker could either thrill or make one grimace. There wasn't a lot of money about in the thirties, and some women weren't too particular about what they put round their nether regions.

Next door's privet hedge was a no man's land. It divided our front garden from theirs. The old mother next door was a chirpy old body dressed in black with a voluminous white apron and strapped buttoned house shoes, white hair always neatly encased in a net. Her daughter was an unsmiling prim, a gloves-and-hat-to-church kind of person who did most of the heavier household chores. She it was who emerged, at times, dressed in heavy gardening gloves and wellingtons, and all she had in mind was to trim the side hedge which was half ours and half hers. A nasty dark green hedge full of woody growth, it needed attack. Snipping, Miss Prim-and-Proper would do exactly her assessed half width and no more, so that the hedge looked like a skinhead's haircut left half done because the scissors broke. "Funny woman," my dad would say. "Why don't she do it all one time and ask me the next?"

"Because she is a wise woman," mum would retort. "Wait for you to do it and the hedge would be half way up the wall to the bedroom window."

Our houses were the sort young kids sketched in chalk on dull dun paper in primary school: front door, window up, window down. I loved 29 Angel as it looked when dad had newly painted the front door, when the hedge had just been trimmed, when the front step was glowing scarlet with freshly applied Cardinal paste (doing this last was one of mum's many chores). When mum was weeding the garden, she often knelt and breathed in deeply before the underside of the front window. There blossomed in purity, sweetness, and brick-eroding tendrils, a climbing shrub of heady jasmine. I can shut my eyes now and recall that scent. The rhapsodic dreams it brought me, of a pink cloud Arabian existence, of a harem of houris, trousered in silks or diaphanous gauzy folds, each one white of bosom, fair of face, and perpetually smiling. I was lost until the fish man's cart rattled by and he bawled out "Fresh herring!" or a distant backfire shattered my reverie as an old banger hit the King Street's poorly set tar-block surface.

Incidents happened in the front garden. Drunks reeling down from the pub ended up in it, on their backs snoring. "How are we going to get rid of him?" mum would fuss. "Don't like the look of him, Sid. Too big and burly." Out went dad with a garden fork. "Sod off quick, or I'll ventilate you, mate, and you'll be breathing through holes in your arse." Dad was never cowardly.

Once, when I was about eleven, I awoke to hear murmurs from the big bedroom. Mum and dad weren't arguing. It sounded more like a discussion. I padded over the dark landing and entered their room. They were at the window, looking down.

"Get away, son," Dad pushed me away. "It's not for your eyes."

I pushed back harder. "Why, it's a couple, and they're…"

"So they are, now get back," Dad said. "The grass must be wet, or they wouldn't be doing it like that, pressing in on my privet hedge, and his backside nearly shoving her through."

He moved swiftly, and, reaching under the bed, he dragged, slid, and hoisted up the piss-pot.

"Sid, you can't!" But mum knew he could, and stepped aside as he raised the window.

The sound of that, loud in the night, must have made the engaged couple jump apart and look up for the source. Just in time, too.

"Dampened you down, has it?" dad roared. "Hoppit, quick, otherwise I'll be down to the kitchen for what I carve the Sunday joint with. You want it slicing off, mate!"

Dad was a man of action. He watched the couple flee, then said to me, "Stay with your mother 'til I get back. I'm going down. I'll find a stick and a torch. That buck rabbit will have left a French letter behind, or I'm a Dutchman. We don't want people thinking we rent the grass out for twitchy arsehole flattening!"

Dad could be crude at times. Mum never. She would tolerate language referring to anyone other than herself, but God help him if dad's wrath spurred him to tack a swear word onto any description of her. "Have you been tidying again, you interfering cow? I can't find this week's *Radio Times*." That was enough. Mum would sulk in retaliation, and she did it so well she would reduce dad to an abject wretch. "When are you going to speak again, girl? It's been three days now." Mum would glare, bang down his dinner in front of him, then sit all evening by the fire and darn. She had a way of mending a hole in a sock as if she were trying to close a gaping wound in her side. I would know how badly dad felt by the way he pretended to read his library book – the fewer pages he flicked over in the course of an hour, the worse he felt.

Mum would time her sulks to last 'til pay day. "I've made you an apple turnover for afters today." It might be a jam roly-poly or a fig pudding boiled in a cloth. The dumb wife war was over.

Let's get inside the house…

Once the front door is closed, and its thick, wide, solid chunk of wood effectively closes off the sounds of the street, one stands in a passage that runs to the back door, unused except when the dustman calls and lugs in the bin from the walled rear garden. Dad tips the dustman well at Christmas, so neither he nor mum will hoick and trundle the bin over the polished linoleum to the front door. "That's his job," says he, and for his toil the dustman gets a bottle of port at Christmas. I like the passage. I sit on the stairs and watch the sunlight streaming through the half-moon fanlight, making the dust motes dance in the gloom.

One picture hangs in the passage. It depicts a group of men gathering about a fire engine, and the ageing, enlarged photograph has their faces a silverfish white and the main tones a yellowing sepia. My mother's father, wide of body and densely thicketed as to beard, dominates the group of volunteer firemen. To show capability, they have uncoiled a hose. One of them directs its nozzle out to the foreground, menacing, gigantic. 'We are men' the photograph records.

The stairs to the bedrooms climb opposite a gas lamp bracket, which serpentines to a white honeycomb mantle that flares incandescent on wintry evenings. It is customary to keep a light in the passage. Not to do so stamps a resident in the street as inhospitable, niggardly, even dead. "I saw your light not on. Wondered if all was well?"

Above the gas lamp, a bell, a real bell shaped like a church bell reduced in size, hangs on a springy metal tongue. Unconnected in any way to motivation outside, it gathers dust, and I inferred without being told that it had once jangled to summon an overworked, poorly paid skivvy, even in these modest dwellings. Wasn't there a box room upstairs, two strides and one-and-a-half toecaps across, originally designed to sleep a domestic? I could imagine this domestic struggling to black-lead the kitchen range with Zebo. The range was a dark satanic beast, its eye a barred fire glowing fiercely. I could picture this poor drudge heating a brick in the range's side oven, then wrapping it in flannel at about midnight to take with her to her freezing bed as a means of warming her feet.

I am not done with the passage. I was never done with the passage, especially on rainy days when not at school. With mum gone off to her 'little job', as she called it (charring in genteel Kensington, making beds for people who actually made beds for the masses in the factory they owned), I could whip up one of the coco-matting doormats and use the stairs for a helter-skelter, squatting on the mat, bumpity-bumping from top landing to passage, the mat sliding out from beneath my bum. I would grip its whiskery hairiness at the sides, bruising my knuckles on the way down, and clouds of dust would rise on my thumping descent. I varied my descent of the stairs to a face-down tobogganing, which caused bristles to unkindly stroke my chin. Those mats! And before mum returned, the passage had to be restored, shiny clean, free from all that dust I'd whacked out to drift and besmirch. Brooming was not enough. I had to get one of the floor cloths and go all over the lino thoroughly. I knew where the Mansion polish was, among the boot brushes and Cherry Blossom shoe polish in the boot-box. It was there for a 'very good reason'. Mum kept everything that polished or cleaned in the boot-box out in the scullery. "A place for everything, and everything in its place," she would say. At the drop of a hat, she mumbled proverbs and old wives' sayings like that, like a predictable juke box turning out the same old unchanged tunes.

There was no lino at the far end of the passage. It cut off, just like that. The flooring changed abruptly from smart shine to dull floorboards. Here ran along the walls either side mounted coatracks,

racks that racked anyone's patience searching for a particular mac or coat, since everything bulged out obese from the wall. It looked, there in shadow, that half a dozen scruffily dressed blokes were hanging in couples, riding piggyback with heads drawn in and legs drawn up. If you wanted a particular coat, it would be there, right on the hook, but below several others seldom or never needed. Coats with holes or rips, with pockets stuffed with scarves and gloves and mittens, macs so stiffened from crease and disuse they resembled unmanageable tent cloth... Nothing was ever thrown away. There was a cap, maker's name side up, showing where a greasy head whiffing of solidified brilliantine had darkened the celluloid over the label. Who wore a cap? Not me. Not dad. Then I remembered. A lodger had left this cap, but had taken instead dad's watch and mum's one good brooch, the gold one with 'MIZPAH' on. We had lodgers the way other people had items slashed off their shopping lists. When we were hard up, mum put a card in the newsagents, stuck up on the back of the door. The lodger was always a man. No temptation for dad.

Chapter 2

Lodgers

Mum first took in a lodger after she and dad had spat and raved in a row over money.

It was not that he couldn't fork out the extra bob or two she needed for socks for me. But he allotted mum a fixed sum each week from his very good wages, so any more dribs and drabs requested from his beer and baccy money meant his temper lost in an instant: "borrow from the insurance"; "ask me later on in the week"; "those socks will take a bit more darning" – he was a fount of excuses for gripping tightly onto his cash. So, mum set her lips and went off to get a lodger. She spread word she had a room vacant for a clean-living, respectable working man. She told the milkman, the old girl who worked in the shop around the corner, the flighty young floozie who worked in the light bulb factory, anyone who might know someone who needed accommodation.

Such a business mum made of interviewing a potential occupant of the second bedroom. "Now, up the stairs and turn left. You see we have installed a gas fire, and the big double bed is for you. I will let you have a key, but I have ears alert even when I'm sleeping, so no sneaking a girl in late and letting her out again early. That's our best washstand. Nice tiles, don't you think? You will get a fresh towel on the roller whenever you ask. Don't smoke in bed. There's a chamber pot under the bed, of course, but I shall expect you to only use that for liquid waste." Mum could put things plainly yet pleasantly when she chose. She also put a price on the room in accordance with what the fellow wore and how his hands revealed either a soft or scarring occupation.

Unfortunately for me, my small box bedroom opened off from the lodger's room, and I know that some of our lodgers got irritated when I had to cut through their bedroom when I went to bed.

Mr. Rooney was the first of our lodgers, a charming, smooth-talking, puckish little man with fair oil-slicked hair and a mouthful of blindingly white, plainly false choppers. He was needy, was Mr. Rooney. "Could I have my jug refilled, dear lady?" he would say. Or, "I wonder if I may have another slice of your excellent buttered toast?" But he was also a borrower. "I am visiting a dear friend of mine in Kentish Town and I only have a ten-shilling note. You couldn't see your way to lending me tenpence for the fare, could you, sweet lady?"

'Never a borrower or a lender be' was one of my mother's wise old sayings, and both she and dad hated the idea of owing money. "Debt is theft," they often said. The borrowings increased until mum had had enough, and off went Mr. Rooney, because mum was, "Having a relative to stay for an indefinite length of time, and I'm sorry but I'm afraid you will have to find lodgings elsewhere."

Our next lodger was a commercial traveller. With his pin-striped black and white suit and sleek black hair, he had the smooth good looks of a 1930s film star, with good real teeth and an easy smile. He arrived in style in a maroon convertible with a black top, which made the kids playing outside gawp with awe and wonder, so few cars were seen in Angel Road. I stood on our doorstep, hoping he would be our next occupant.

"I understand there's a room vacant here, sonny."

That 'sonny' annoyed me, but I forgave him. He would lend a touch of class to number 29, and that car standing outside would surely impress the other kids in our street.

In his middle thirties, Norman sloshed and burbled in front of the washstand, using copious drenchings of water from the jug, and shaving to pinkly scraped perfection his slightly chubby features. He was vague as to which firms he represented, and seldom revealed where his travels led. I began to think that Norman pushed scent or some form of cosmetics, or stockings or undies, maybe, because Norman certainly attracted females like a magnet attracts iron filings. How Norman's girlfriends wanted to cling! They knocked for and demanded to see him, girls in their teens and older women. Mum would sniff and criticise when she had informed them that Norman was out, and, no, she did not know when he would be back. "Don't like the look of that last one," she would say. "All bright red lipstick and dyed peroxide hair. Says she's come all the way from Alperton to see him. That's a long ride on the tube."

'Not quite the long ride on a tube she was looking for,' I thought to myself with a quiet grin.

For some months Norman sold his wares secretly and sang in his room while buttoning down the fine shirts mum sent to the laundry for him. "He's so smart, so refined, such a gentleman," she would say. 'So deceitful,' I'd say to myself. Mum could not wake up to the havoc he was causing in the district, and a wide district at that, considering it had brought a woman all the way from respectable Alperton. She had to be respectable – Alperton was all 'I'm on my way to the tennis club old chap, bring the dear lady wife round for cocktails next Thursday and we'll dance to the radiogram'.

Norman went as the smell of compost blows away in the wind. He packed up hastily one night as we were getting ready for bed, and came down as mum was handing me my nightlight and a warm brick wrapped in flannel to warm up my cold sheets. He had money in his hand. He spoke, distraught, a rush of words, and the pink chubby face screwed itself up into anxious writhings. "I'm sorry, I must leave at once for personal reasons. Take this, a week's rent in compensation for the inconvenience. Goodbye and thanks for everything…"

The black overcoat was thrust on, the front door clicked and shut (eased closed, not slammed). A gentleman to the last.

Not long after that, a young girl called. She had missed a period and was now missing Norman in her pathetic, trusting life. She wailed on the doorstep while mum sympathised, and realised how little she knew of Norman. "What was his firm? He hadn't actually said. What was his last name? Well, we have a name, but it might not be his real name, he might have lied. The number of his car? Well, that was funny, no one had thought to note it down, I'm sure. Best come in for a cup of tea, get settled a little in your mind before you go home. There, there, don't take on so my dear."

Norman had left behind a partly used jar of hair cream. Something else he had partly used and now thrown away.

Our next paying guest was Henry Hughes, a thin, bespectacled clerk who worked in a shipping office. He lugged upstairs so many suitcases of different shapes and sizes that dad joked that he must have stolen a ship and was hoarding the disassembled parts to put together later. As soon as the flow of cargo was safely installed in his room, he approached mum. "Would it disturb anyone if I typed of an evening in my room?"

"What's going on up there?" Dad was the first to speculate irritably. A succession of nights had gone by with our latest invader shooting up the stairs after the customary cup of tea and pleasantries. The tapping of the keys wasn't so bad, but every time he reached the end of a row, the typewriter bell would ding before he typed along to the next line. Then came enlightenment. Bearing in the crook of his arm a number of cardboard folders, Henry beamed patronisingly upon us all sitting in the kitchen. Would we like to hear a line or two of his latest play? He hadn't yet been able to interest theatrical circles into putting one of his efforts into production, but this latest brainchild was a certain winner, and we must hear it and marvel. Will you please settle and pin back your ears?

We soon wished we had pinned 'Do Not Disturb' on the kitchen door instead. The soft monotonous voice droned on and on. The play was a period piece, unbelievable in its banality and in its ridiculously wrong dialogue for the century it was supposed to embrace, the Eighteenth. Characters exploded with 'gadzooks' and 'odds fish' and 'prithees' on every page.

"May I kiss thee, Mistress Tremayne?" I shall never forget that line, or the timid damsel's reply: "Fie, Sir Fortescue, I have known thee but a 'ennight."

Where was Henry dreaming up this balderdash? The plot was as thin as a vagrant's vest: penniless young buck woos pretty damsel; irate damsel's dad is convinced he is after her fortune; rich great uncle in Venezuela dies and leaves the young buck a fortune anyway; and they all live happily ever after. And this hackneyed diatribe was expected to grip an audience!

It didn't grip dad. I could see his glance straying to the evening paper, open at the wireless page. To stem the spate flowing from Henry's lips, Mum hastily asked, "How does it end?"

He told her. "What do you think? Original, don't you agree?" Henry's eyes shone bright with the glow of an author enraptured with his own work.

Dad said, polite but insincere, "A nice tale, pleasant, should be entertaining."

As Henry's glance went back to the page, Mum shocked us all by suddenly saying, "It's not very good, I'm afraid."

If she had tossed a bomb into Henry's lap, he would not have been any more alarmed. First he went pink, then white, and then his anger manifested itself in attack. "I should have known better. What would you people know of the theatre?"

"Quite a lot," Mum said coldly. "My husband is distantly related to the Randalls, the theatrical family, and although you wouldn't know it, he has been on the stage himself in his younger days." That was as an eccentric dancer, but Henry didn't need to know that. "I think I know what would charm theatregoers, and what you have before you wouldn't. It's too light. No weight to it, Mr. Hughes. I have seen Matheson Lang and Sir John Martin Harvey at the King's Theatre here, and any number of excellent plays at the Lyric. I love a good play. That's my point. It wouldn't be right to let you go on hammering your play to the end. Personally, I wanted you to end its unfolding after the first couple of minutes."

A deathly silence fell upon the kitchen scene. Then Henry, his face showing chagrin and hostility mixed, went upstairs, and he came down the next morning with the coolest of daily greetings. Shortly afterwards, he left.

Dad must have relented and given mum more from his wage packet after that, because we had no more lodgers after Henry's departure and we were left in peace. At least, that was the case until a couple of years later, when a female relative of my dad's was thrown out of her bedsit for smoking in bed and pleaded to be allowed to occupy our spare bedroom.

If other lodgers had been a thorn in my side and an irritation to me, considering the close proximity of my bedroom to theirs, they were nothing compared to the nuisance that was Maggie.

Maggie was still a keen smoker. She smelled permanently of tobacco, the aroma of which she attempted to hide under a liberal sprinkling of *Evening in Paris* perfume. In my small adjoining bedroom, I had a nightlight with a few matches beside it, in case a stray draught blew it out in the night. Maggie would rap on my door, then open it without waiting for a 'come in' and appear in the doorway with a voluminous nightie draped over her ample body, which appeared pink and chunky beneath the diaphanous folds. "Got any matches?" she would ask, and then she would sweep in and take them from the mantelpiece without asking.

In her mid-thirties, but admitting to gracing this earth for only twenty-nine summers, Maggie fancied herself as God's gift to men. She owned a luxurious head of naturally waving copper-gold hair. Her body curved voluptuously. Her bosom was firm, big, and deliberately covered in blouses so shiny and tight that blokes' mouths gaped as they sucked in breath on seeing it. Employed as a counter-hand in one of Joe Lyons' tea shops, a mere swabber of surfaces and server of slopped cuppas from a steaming urn, she gave herself the airs of a duchess born to dominate lesser beings.

Maggie immediately made it known that, among the multitude of things she disapproved of, her baptismal name featured prominently. She would answer to 'Penny', a pretty name, in her far from humble opinion. "When a gentleman caller comes here, you will call me Penny," she told us, and so, to avoid any unpleasantness, we complied. The men who called for Maggie were foolishly fascinated by her, and invariably smart, with good jobs. Some even had cars.

She spoke of them scathingly. "All mugs, they are. I'll get what I can from them; they'll get nothing from me. One day, my Len will come back, and if I find anyone better than him, well, yes, I'll think about getting married, but I don't think I'll ever find one like him."

My mother sighed. Several years before, Maggie had met Len, an ordinary bloke who worked as a supervisor in Osram's light bulb factory. Nice enough, polite, but so ordinary that my mum and dad had never understood what she saw in him. 'Average' described him perfectly. Average build, average height, and with a slightly wrinkled face and slightly distorted mouth which gave him a permanently ironic and unintentional grin. Maggie adored him. She would speak incessantly of their inevitable marriage – the wedding dress she wanted, what kind of flowers she would have in her bouquet, etc. – so that when she visited us, my dad would make some excuse to go out into the garden. A loose brick in the garden wall urgently needed replacing, or the wireless aerial was playing up and he needed to see what was wrong.

One day, Len had told Maggie, "Don't ask me any questions, but I will have to go away for a while and it may be for quite a long time. But remember this, Maggie: one day I will come back for you, I promise. But if you ever meet anyone that you love better than me, you have my blessing to be happy." Then he had left abruptly, leaving Maggie to collapse on the doorstep in floods of tears. A concerned neighbour had got in touch with my mum. Maggie was in a state. She would not eat. She was unkempt, scruffy, not wearing her usual mask of thick make-up. She had let herself go. Mum gently tried to persuade her, in the nicest possible way, that she had been dumped. Maggie was having none of it. "No, no, he loves me!" she wailed. "There has to be a good reason." After several weeks of constant tears, Maggie finally decided to pull herself together. It was then that she adopted the hard exterior. Until she found Mr. Right, she would retain an arms-length relationship with the men she went out with, seldom yielding, and then only to suffer a brief embrace.

My dad did not have much sympathy. "She's like a bloody heroine from a romantic opera. 'One fine day, he'll come back to me!' Why can't she just accept that he dumped her but tried to soften the blow?"

I was in the Army when he did come back. I heard it all from my mum, who was so impressed with the romantic improbability of it all that she never tired of telling the story again and again. There had been a knock at the door. Mum was busy in the kitchen, and Maggie, now our lodger, had opened the door to reveal Len standing there. Maggie had screamed, fallen on the floor and burst into tears. There had been crying, laughing, and intermingled cries of "I told you I'd come back!"

and "I knew you would!" and then Maggie and Len had gone upstairs to her room and didn't emerge until two hours later, both crying excitedly, "We're getting married!"

Unlike *Madam Butterfly*, there was a happy ending for Maggie. Len made a model husband, we were told. He conscientiously flicked ash into the numerous ash trays, worked overtime to get Maggie the smart new furniture she wanted, and took her for regular holidays to Skegness or Southend-on-Sea. There was one proviso: she was never to ask where he had been in those intervening years. She agreed. Their new house was only six doors down from ours, and she tended both the house and garden with loving care. I remember the wonderful and overpowering powdery smell of the night-scented stocks in her garden when I returned home. "Such a lovely happy ending," said my mum. "You couldn't make it up."

Chapter 3

The Front Room

On any ordinary weekday, the thought of entering the front room of 29 Angel was as unthinkable as the spinster next door dancing the can-can without knickers. There should have been a notice on the door reading, 'KEEP OUT! THIS MEANS YOU!'

The very door of this best room in the house promised elegance within. The panels of the door were painted a spotless magnolia with a surround of Carson's Signal Red Gloss. Shove the door inwards, and one breathed in the scent of wax lavender polish rising from the Art Deco sideboard, its doors embellished with a carved sunflower pattern. On the wall was a hand-coloured photograph of Geishas in patterned silk kimonos, gracefully leaning over a bridge. The front room lino was a blood-red, gleaming sea, on which floated symmetrically-positioned squares of genuine Wilton. Like an island in this sea was the oval mahogany table, its mirror-like surface covered with a white damask cloth printed with bunches of purple grapes.

This hallowed retreat was only inhabited by us on Sundays, at Christmas, and when relatives called. The relaxed easiness of weekday living was left outside the door as we entered this room on the Lord's day. Mum expected us to drop the tone of our voices to a well-modulated softness. A weak fire burned in the grate. "Well," mum would say, "it is only to be lit on a Sunday, and we don't want any mountains of ash to be cleared away on Monday morning. It might make the room dirty."

Cold comfort Rexine armchairs chilled the back in the front room. These days, Rexine would be called 'faux leather'. The synthetic material was amazingly cold.

There was a mausoleum-like sanctity about the front room. "Don't disturb the runner on the sideboard." "No, you may not have a glass of home-made wine, young drunkard in the making! Ask your father tomorrow."

Sanctimonious Sundays! I rise from the iceberg clutch of my chair and sprawl on the sofa, a similarly cool couch, and it is as if the long hand of a cadaver is feeling along the underpart of my thigh.

"Get up from there at once!" says mum. "That's what's wrong with this room – you make it untidy!"

"Four o'clock gone, my girl," says dad, contemplating his pocket watch. "Time for tea."

Tea on Sundays was a feast. On the transfer-printed blue and white flowered large plate in the centre of the table resided shrimp sandwiches on brown bread, or cheese and tomato, if you preferred. There were small glass dishes of winkles and another plate of plain brown bread to accompany them. A glass vase bought for the purpose did not contain flowers but leafy sticks of celery. And to follow that was fruit jelly with Carnation milk. Finally, mum had made a cake, caraway seed cake usually, or jam sponge or fruit cake, all washed down with tea from the pewter tea pot.

"How about the gramophone for an hour?" said mum after tea. Mum looked at me. "I want newspaper under it and no scratches on the table. Don't throw any used gramophone needles in the fireplace. If there's a good needle fitted already, make sure you pick off any bits of fluff before very carefully putting the record on. Choose something nice. See the sound thing isn't along to the loud end. I'm not deaf and neither is your father. Remember, it's not a barrel organ, although you are a monkey at times."

I wanted to hear Elsie Carlisle liven things up with her brassy rendering of 'Ain't it Grand to be Bloomin' Well Dead' – I ached to hear about the coffin with its 'bloomin' great 'andles' – but instead I had to settle for Count John McCormack tenoring through 'Macushla' until I wished that he would take the next boat across the sea to Ireland and leave me in peace.

Then, another dreaded moment came: mum predictably requesting, "Play my favourite. If there were words to it, they would be so sad..." So, reluctantly I put on 'In a Monastery Garden'. As the violin scrapings start to sound, I mentally make up a poem to fit the tune...

Oh, this room is bloody freezing
Wish I'd long trousers to hide cold knees in
We have winkles on a Sunday
Wish I could have them on a Monday

The invisible 'behave' instruction only came down in the front room at Christmas. At Christmas, anything went except tearing the paper from the walls. Brazil nut and cobnut shells littered the fireplace, were trodden into the Wilton mats, and scored the waxen lino, but mum said not a word. Yellow paper hat turned sideways on her head, she helped add to the debris, silver nutcrackers crunching, splitting, demolishing... "Oh, this one's a fraud! Nothing inside but emptiness!" "Sid, give me over the Fuller's chocolates." "Is that my glass or yours?" And she beamed like a lighthouse lit up. She had been at the port, tried the ginger wine, and had now risen to seek the lime juice to mildly flavour her glass of gin. When a drooping line of paper chains came loose from the ceiling and fell across her nose, she flung the links from her and brightly caterpillared amongst the nutshells as if seeking for bits undiscovered. "Leave them there. It will all get cleared up ... sometime."

Mum didn't care. Jovially, she grabbed dad by the waist and began humming, and they renewed half-forgotten glides performed on the dance floor of their youth. She pressed her ample belly on dad's even more generous paunch, and they bumped into furniture like Tweedledum and Tweedledee, until mum would realise how breathless and flushed she had become. Eventually, she collapsed into an armchair, where she fanned herself with anything handy, probably the pinny she wore like a drudge's badge. This one would be a present from unimaginative dad, who always sent her an enormous card on festive or anniversary occasions, all silver glitter dust and bunched flowers and romantic words, but also always presented her with a gift deplorably useful.

Soon dad lit a fat cigar, and mum followed him about, sniffing the rich aroma. He would choke, his welling eyes sharply stung. "No, it's fine. You never forget to get me one, do you, my girl? Come on, let's play 'Chase the Ace'. 'Pontoon'? Right, I'll be banker." The pile of halfpennies at his elbow rose, his eyes narrowed in greed.

Dad got very grumpy when he lost. A sullen look over-swept his meaty red face, he stabbed out his cigar, and belted wood bruises out of his chair in thumping it with agitated bottom shifting. "My luck will change, it must do." "Are you both *still* sticking?" "After this round I'm out – too tired." "Anyone want tea, after all the stuff we've poured down our gullets tonight?"

I'd hear him chinking up the total of what he had won. He had slipped out into the passage to count it. Dad was like that. In generous mood, he'd change a ten bob note to buy me a lemonade and Abernethy biscuit on a Sunday morning riverbank stroll, the side with the pubs on. Yet there were endless arguments about new clothes or shoes for me. "New shoes already? He can't have worn them out yet. What? His feet have grown? Well, he'll have to wear plimsolls indoors to save on the leather with the next pair."

Boxing Day was agony in the front room. The fire blazed just as merrily, but all heart had gone from the male revellers. There we sat, dad and I, in miserable awareness that dinner meant the remains of the turkey, all picked ribs, flaky leavings, and bits of sage stuffing.

"Buck up, you two," Mum would say, surveying us with lacklustre eyes. "This isn't a fine time for me, you know. The place is a pigsty, and if you two hadn't both been pigs yesterday I could serve up a decent meal. As it is, I may have to open a tin of corned beef!"

Dad sat up abruptly, unshaven, and still resentful because the postman hadn't thanked him for his seasonal tip. "If you think I'm going to eat congealed South American muck after yesterday's feast, you can think again! I'll have all the leftover mince pies for my dinner. And let's have a respectful silence for my fat head. Make some coffee, and take this bugger into the scullery with you. Scavenger, he is. He's licked his fingers ninety-eight times finishing off the Turkish delight, those ashes in the grate are what's left of the Fuller's chocolate box, and that grin on his face is a sticky one. What with crystallised ginger, dates, and the dregs of the crème de menthe, your guts, son, must be a fermenting vat."

The Salvation Army invaded the street sometimes on Boxing Day, and dad glowered at them through the window. "Haven't they got any homes? Disturbing the peace with their oompahs and tambourine jingling. Here I am, wanting a nap, and a flock of black crows descend. Look at that bonneted virgin bustling up the steps opposite with the collecting box. If she knocks here, we're out. Tell your mother not to clatter anything, or she'll have to go to the door with her purse."

"Sid, it's Christmas," mum said reproachfully. "We should give something. Remember those less fortunate than ourselves."

"Suppose we are fortunate," agreed dad, reluctantly relenting. "All right. Give them a bob when they knock."

When the Christmas season ended, the front room soon glistened again. And the front room door remained firmly closed until the following Sunday. Unless any stray relatives decided to visit…

Chapter 4

Relatives

My, we had some weird relations calling at 29 Angel. To protect any distant descendants who may be living somewhere in the universe, I have changed their names, but not their habitually irritating characteristics...

Two or three times a year, Uncle Ned came to foul up our front room. Anyone having Ned for a brother should have booted his father to the far end of the street. He was my dad's surviving brother – their younger brother, gentle and polite Fred, had been killed in the Battle of the Somme.

Ned prided himself on his prowess at darts. He arrived, stinking of beer, and at once relived games he had won at 'The Doves', where he was uncrowned champion. It was said he could cover the dartboard with a sheet of paper and still artfully spike any number, double or treble, or even the bullseye.

He also caught fish. We got hour long accounts of dull afternoons spent by the side of a murky canal. He told of us of water in his waders, the one that got away, and sometimes we even got a couple of his captures ourselves. Dace, bream, whatever they were, they all tasted like the mud at the bottom of the canal.

Ned was straight-backed and as tall as a guardsman. He sported a virile man's boldly bristled moustache, waxed at either end à la Hercule Poirot, although Ned did not have that character's Gallic charms. But Ned thought he was a ladies' man. He eyed mum a lot, and never mind dad resenting the mental undressing. We all knew Ned's motive for the visit. At last he'd rise to go, and somehow, by dogged persuasion of actual handling, he'd manoeuvre mum into the passage. I have never fathomed why dad stood for this blatant flirting. He knew Ned's next move would be to pin mum against the passage wall. We waited, tense, for the sound of the smacking kiss. I daren't look at dad. I experienced humiliation, rage, and a mild despair. How could dad let Ned kiss her like that? She would have to endure a rush of beer fumes, those greedy wet lips, her own crushed in the smother of that awful moustache, yellowed from the hand-rolled cigarettes that oft had Ned coughing, saliva coated tongue thrust out. Uncle Ned was a pincher of bottoms, a leaner in crowded Underground carriages. He had a deep gurgling laugh occasioned by a sense of his own imagined manliness. It wasn't a man that had mum sneak, embarrassed and red-cheeked, back into the kitchen – she had been kissed by a beast.

We all sat shamefaced whenever dad's youngest sister, Lil, left whatever man she was living with at the time and came to show us that she still knew how to rouge up her cheeks and paint on a smile.

Lil would sing in the outside khazi, proving that a near-tart like her could still enjoy life to the full, her shrill notes floating over the gap at the top of the lavvy door in such merry escape you would have thought she was expelling all the joy in her heart as well as whatever else she had no further use for. "Nance!" she called, using mum's affectionate nickname. "There's no paper out here! Bring us a bit of *The News of the World* so I can have something interesting to read!" Hoots of laughter then issued from Lil's carmined lips. "Oh, you know me, I can see the funny side of everything!"

A word on Aunt Lil: she was younger than dad, but by how many years? She was archly reticent about her years, always inviting people to guess. That their guesses in the main both pleased and flattered says a lot for Lil's way of living. She sang and sailed through numerous short-lived affairs, all of which apparently left her emotionally unscarred. Lil had a large bosom fronting a larger heart. She would love anyone, given a chance, irrespective of age and sex. It was a crying shame that she seemed to attract inarticulate men of a brooding aspect, menially employed, for the most part, and one might have thought she chose them for their rough, scored, big hands. I do mean big. Lil's blokes had hands as big as a traffic policeman's white glove, although their hands were not so pristine.

Mum and I once went to see Lil in a couple of rooms she was disgracing with her current amour. She had the living room a pit, typically arranged as throw anything anywhere. Her man sat forward in a salvaged armchair with its seat collapsed, looking as if an assailant had pushed him into a handy coffin. His long arms and banana bunch fingers draped over the armchair sides, and, tired as he was at the time, he looked as if he had given up the struggle to get out. It was obvious he didn't want any visitors. He greeted mum and me with a reluctant nod. I recall the scruffy table had half a loaf on it, and a pot of jam to keep it company. Lil's clothes – jumpers, knickers, slips – were strewn on anything above floor level. If she had stripped naked at a jumble sale, determined to try on the lot, she would have achieved a like scene. Yet Lil made our afternoon delightful with her cries of joy at seeing us, and she even coaxed a smile out of the ape sitting in the sorry armchair. "Don't mind him, he doesn't say much. You are all right, aren't you, Nance?"

The best way I can find of describing Lil was as 'radiantly dowdy'. She always threw her clothes on, zips half-fastened, maybe a button missing. Her frocks were youthful, her blouses riotously floral or lacy-fussy, invariably too tight and straining. Her hats were the worst thing about her. She had fluffy, fair hair and a trusting china doll's gentle blue eyes, and I always thought the shapeless felt hats she wore spoiled her forever young-at-heart image, much too respectable for her flighty character.

If Lil was my favourite female relative, the uncle I liked best was Uncle Jack.

My uncle Jack was a card – the jack of spades. Mum's brother, he was dark, and shadowed all over his rough-hewn face with the craters left by a childhood smallpox eruption. A docker on the wharf down

Fulham way, he worked in the malty air wafting from Manbré & Garton's sugar refinery, and so the smell of caramel wafted from Uncle Jack. He would call in after humping hundredweight sacks, a wide leather belt keeping his thick, hairy trousers up over boots with steel toecaps. There was no messing with Jack, no politeness or striving for mannered ways. Jack's idea of the good life was a shilling each way on a dead cert, brown ale, Billy Bennett's smutty monologues at Shepherd's Bush Empire, a knotted, red-spotted handkerchief over his head as he sat tilted back in a Southend deckchair, and jellied eels in a basin every now and then.

There was much love that flowed between mum and her brother. I liked him. I admired him for his 'simple working man trying to graft a crust' image, for his perky Cockney 'can't get me down' persistence. Saucered his tea, did Jack. Blew on it if it was scalding, and sucked it down.

Jack was given to throwing up whatever job he had for impulsive ventures. His bookstall in Shepherd's Bush Market was doomed to failure mainly because Jack was not the most literate of men and could not advise customers as to the gist of the story of most books. They came to read for free and would lean against one side of the stall reading for ages without paying so much as a penny. The next venture was The Penny Grocer. This consisted of Jack buying various household items in bulk, like raisins, ginger, tea, sugar and pepper, and putting them into little packets, for which he charged a penny. From this, he was supposed to make a profit. I used to help him make up his little packets.

How many we filled, Jack and I, it's impossible to remember, but this scheme was doomed to failure from the start, too. Jack carried the items in a lidded case that weighed a ton. It fastened round his neck with straps, Jack a cart horse in rig. I went around the doors with him. It was mortifying. I tried to keep optimistic to keep up his spirits.

"Why should I buy from you when I can get a big packet of tea from Palmers?" they'd say. "Works out cheaper in the end, that way." And the door would be slammed. The truth of this couldn't be denied. Or, "Go away, con-man!" This was unfair. It was Jack who had been conned. For every three women who bought, twenty did not want to know, so Jack, with those wretched little packets left over, eventually gave them to mum, and went back to offloading wharf barges.

Clara Cluck was Jack's wife. We saw her seldom, and hardly ever with him. I think he was a bit ashamed of her. She was louder and more raucous than him. The nickname suited her. She kept up a continuous stream of chatter, and bustled round like a busy old hen, offering her unwanted help to my long-suffering mum.

"Now I am here, ducks, you must let me help you with getting the tea ready." "Cutting bread and butter, are you? I can do that." "Oh, I must tell you about what you are envying on my coat – you know I just love pretty bits of jewellery."

Clara always had some kind of insect crawling across her coat. Not the living kind, but perhaps a spider picked out in mosaic bricks, or an enamel ladybird in black and red. But I did like the fake diamond butterfly with sapphire eyes.

"Let me tell you how I came by this. You know the man who keeps the second hand goods business around the corner? He wanted three and six for this. I ask you! Three and six! Guess how much I managed to beat him down to. Go on, Nance, guess!"

Mum didn't really care, but politely pretended to. She had to be nice to Clara for Jack's sake. Jack was her only surviving sibling – three sisters had died in early childhood.

"Well, I suppose you have to be grateful for all the relatives you can get," she observed, somewhat strangely. But, apart from Jack and Lil, I could have done without the others.

Chapter 5

Attempting to Make Friends

My face did not please me.

Whenever I left 29 Angel for school, someone would remark on my features and laugh. In their opinion, I bore a youthful resemblance to one Joe. E. Brown (later of *Some Like It Hot* fame), a popular comedian of the day, who made a jackass of himself in every picture he strode through, mostly in wide white trousers and yachting blazers. I could not see the likeness myself, although I looked for it in the mirror. How dare folks think I had a mouth as wide as that goon's? He had a way of yawing open his mouth and suddenly closing it in mimicry of a Venus fly trap snapping on a bug, and at the moment of snapping appearing winsome and shy and supposedly lovable all at once. I couldn't stand Joe E. Brown, and to class me with him was a smarting insult.

Of course, both of my parents thought of me as Stan the super-handsome. "He's going to be so tall when he finishes growing," Mum cooed. She spoke about me as if I were a bush in the garden – 'wait 'til it blooms and we'll stand back and marvel'. Dad marked each inch I attained on the wallpaper in indelible pencil. "Stand there, son. Back up straight. We'll make a soldier of you yet." That would start mum spitting sparks, her eyes lit up, furious. She would never release her boy to have his head shot off or stumble about the land glazed and shell-shocked like the poor miserable wretches left over from the '14-'18 war. I knew she was thinking of the wrecked-forever men who sold matches in King Street, or who sang, in no voice worth listening to, the saddest ballad they could think of to charm coppers from the women's purses: men who dragged their feet along the gutters, men with upturned and sightless eyes, often in shoddy rags, men struggling for an identity in a small uniformed troop, where the little chap who wasn't capable of playing anything shook the collecting box under your nose. Mum would bury me alive under the floorboards before she saw me coughing and hawking my lungs up above the informative chunk of cardboard that read, 'GAS VICTIM, PLEASE HELP'.

So, my parents thought me good looking, but they were alone in thinking that. My hair stuck up straight, wouldn't maintain a parting, and was the colour of old string that had been handled a lot. My nose was like a pear drop of putty, gently flattened, then stuck on, showing more nostril than was desirable. And I had spots that would come and go like shy girls got blushes. Picture me emerging from my gate to the sight of kids of both sexes playing. The girls stopped turning rope and chanting 'salt, vinegar, mustard, pepper' and giggled. They were looking at me: my long white legs, by no means sturdy, running up to the shortest of short trousers; my meagre, ferret-like chest encased in some subdued shade of wool pullover; and my sticky-up distemper-brush hair and blob of a nose.

"Why, it's Joe E. Brown! Saw you last week at the Empire. Open your mouth like he does and shut it quick, go on! Hee-hee! All right, don't, then. Rotten sod!"

I would make for Ravenscourt Park on a Sunday afternoon when I should have been at Sunday school. There, I would envy the young blokes wearing 'fifty bob tailor' suits and green spray leafed carnations in their buttonholes, who wandered after the girls who always walked along so slowly that it was obvious they wanted the lads to catch up with them. But there I was, all knobbly knees and pimples and stupid short trousers more befitting a kid of seven. If I so much as smiled at a girl on her own, she might say, "Who you staring at, little lad? Come back in five years' time, when your mum lets you out of your rompers."

A conspiracy existed to keep me as young as possible for as long as possible. If I got hold of some solid brilliantine to slick down my hair, mum would order me to shampoo it out at once. And if it wasn't blazing outside, I always had to wear my school cap to keep my head warm.

Dad was no help.

"Dad, they've got a sale on at Orton's. Could I have my first pair of long-'uns?"

"What do you think, girl?" He'd be studying a blueprint for a wireless on the build. His mind was on raising the garden aerial and getting Toulouse or Mexico.

"Not yet." Mum frowned, and, to show determination, clattered the knives and forks loudly when clearing away. "When he's fourteen. Not before."

"You heard, son." And the old man would follow a circuit with his thick workman's finger, his brains full of ohms, and resistances and grid leaks, and never a considerate thought about it being high time the obscenities of my long skinny white legs were decently veiled from view.

Mum wondered where I had got to if I was out of the house for more than an hour. That was the bane of my existence, and would continue to be so until I reached the magical age of fourteen. Until then, all my time in outside escape had to be accounted for in detail.

"Where did you go?" "Who were you with?" "He's not a nice boy to associate with. He swears a lot, and it's catching, like measles." "I saw you talking to one of the Waites girls, and everybody knows they'll end up like their mother – married at sixteen and nearly had their Brenda in the vestry." "Don't go down by the river! I know you venture there at low tide. You could fall in." "I hear Brian James has got spots. Pimples, you say? Well, to be on the safe side, don't play at his end of the street." "No, you can't go out. It's nine o'clock and all respectable boys are in by then." The embargos were numerous.

"Let's see those hands," she'd say, as if I wasn't capable of washing them myself at the sink. "What have you been at? Dabstones? Or marbles in the gutter?" Her large, brown eyes took on a pained look. "You roam the back alleys like a regular muckworm. There's gobs and phlegm and dogs' stuff and pee about, but down you go, squatting there, flicking cigarette cards, and scraping up the winnings from your little games, and Heaven knows what you scrape up with them. Germs, dirt… And look at your fingernails! One of these days, you'll be the death of me with your filthy ways."

Mum embarrassed me no end in the street. I mean, there I'd be, taking part in a nice, innocent game of 'Releasey-Oh!' or some such, when up she'd pop to interfere. 'Releasey-Oh!' was a game for two teams, and each side had to try to capture a victim from the other. When caught, the victim was pinned against a wall, and the rest of his side had to attempt to crash through a barrier of arms to release him, crying 'Releasey-Oh!' as they did so. It was a tough game, bruise-making, potentially limb-fracturing, although I never knew that happen. So, anyway, the game would be in progress when I was seized by the scruff of the neck. But mum wouldn't address me. No. She fixed any boy other than me there with a dark scowl and said, "I don't want Stanley penned like that. Neither do I want him quaking indoors because he's broken someone's arm. Be warned! Leave Stanley out when choosing sides." And only then would she turn her attention to me. "Now, Stan…" And then she dusted dust from my jacket, inspected my knees, straightened my collar, and adjusted to neat formation and position my tie. Always, I had to wear a tie. She then fiddled with my hair, tidying and patting. And then came the insulting finale to the demeaning encounter. From her handbag or a pocket of her coat, mum produced a handkerchief, a woman's embroidered one, feebly spat on it, and removed imaginary grubby marks from my face.

Despite all this humiliation, whenever sitting gloomy with my elbows on those still bare knees, I would urge mum to let me out to play for a while, and rocketed out into the street to freedom when permission was granted. That is almost literally the way I shot into the street, over the road full pelt, veering in a sweeping half circle and finally stopping in front of the gather of boys, with eyes keen and nostrils a-flare. I demanded with almost fanatical eagerness participation in whatever was going on.

Adults watching my behaviour would mumble, "That boy's half daft, the way he carries on. They're only swapping comics, not dishing out stolen half crowns."

"I'll go in goal," I volunteered, if football was on, with a lamppost for one goalpost and a pile of coats by the wall for another. "I'll run back and get all my *Hotspur* and *Wizard* comics. I'll give two for any of yours." I took the unwanted jobs, I gave odds in favour, I crawled, pleaded and shouted for them to let me be their friend. But the boys who played in the street were resentful of mummy's darling. They eyed me up and down with hostility, plainly contemptuous, ready to punch my arms, push, barge or spit upon me at any excuse, or none. I got in on games fast and tough for the express purpose of letting them do me some damage. Anything to prove that I was tough like them.

"Hey, Tinsley! What you doing falling down like that? Shoulder you down? Never! Must have been the invisible man!" "I wouldn't read one of your comics if it still had the free plastic whistle in it.

Scarper! Go on! Amscray! Get up your own end of the road!"

The point about their rejection of me was a minor class war. Angel Road had an architectural admixture of dwellings: our terraced in-between houses well-kept and with neat front gardens; the posh houses opposite, three-storeyed with attic and basement and steps leading up to the porched front door; and the mean and neglected one-time fishermen's cottages at the far end of the street. These last now housed the low paid, the lazy and the workshy. Slatterns with soiled aprons slumped, arms akimbo, in open doorways, down that end, and the arms akimbo were meaty and grey at the elbows. The younger urchins wore their older brothers' and sisters' worn cast-offs, and wiped their snotty noses on their sleeves.

"Stanley, you are not to go to that end of the street, you hear me? If you play with boys from that end of the street, you might come home with dickies in your hair, and I've always wanted you to be turned out looking nice. Why can't you play with that nice boy Hilary from the houses opposite? You can ask him to come to tea, if you like." This was mum, ever watchful.

Hilary was a nice boy, pleasant and polite. Once he had ventured out to play in the street. Only once. If the other boys gave me a bad time, it was nothing to how they treated him. With hands on hips and exaggeratedly refined accents, they called, "Oh Hilary, Hilary, my dear, have you come to play with us? Would you like a nice game of tennis Hilary? Bleedin' girl's name, Hilary. Go back home to mummy, Hilary, my darling. You're not going to play with us!"

He went back home in tears. I could have made a friend of him, given him some of my comics, even gone to the library with him, or Ravenscourt Park, or down by the river. Of course, I didn't. I didn't dare. I would have lost whatever modicum of street cred I had with the others. I had not the courage to make Hilary my friend.

Chapter 6

Exacting Revenge

I have always hated injustice. There is fair criticism and there is unfair criticism, and the latter needed just retribution. People must not be allowed to get away with casual hurtful insults, insults that would prey on my mind, giving way to much self-analysis and sleeplessness.

"You're too sensitive," mum would say. "Don't let it worry you. 'Sticks and stones may break my bones but calling cannot hurt me.'"

But it did worry me. Physical injuries of the bruising kind that I endured when roughly pushed over by street boys were soon forgotten, but an insult was not, and had to be avenged.

I particularly recall exacting payment from a determinedly middle-class lady who queened it in the refined echelons of Bridge Avenue, just around the corner from us, and opposite the red-bricked apartments known as 'mansions'. The lady in question was usually seen with a clipped poodle of Parisian pomposity in its prancing daintiness and elegant stepping.

One day, I happened to approach this woman in the narrow alleyway leading between Angel Road and her domain, and there occurred that awkward gauche pas-de-deux, when two people try to avoid each other on the same few confining flagstones. She stepped one way, so did I, and in the sudden confusion I was confronted by a snob seemingly owning the street. Then she corrected her move to get out of my way, and guess who inadvertently copied that move?

"Get out of my way, dirty boy!"

The command was spitefully delivered, rapped out sharp, her humourless blue eyes glacially glinting. I wouldn't have minded the order; it was the 'dirty boy' I objected to. Hadn't I not long left home after a thorough wash, my clothes cleanly put on? Dirty!? I was not even faintly grubby: no neck tidemarks; ears clean; shoes shining, as were the soaped surfaces of my skin. She would have to pay for this undeserved insult. I lost sleep hatching a plot. Post a dog turd through her letterbox? Insufficient punishment. That soon could be cleared away, and not even by her, probably, but by some put-upon cleaning lady. To comfort myself, I wandered forlornly into the scullery, where mum was washing a few smalls.

"Mum," I asked. "Can I have a treacle sandwich?" Treacle was a comfort food. I always liked to make my treacle sandwiches myself. I liked opening the tin and getting the knife and watching the lovely thick liquid trickle slowly and glutinously back into the tin and make figures of eight and patterns with the sticky viscous trail. "Well?" mum would always say. "Are you going to make yourself a sandwich, or just play with the stuff all day?"

So, I made myself a treacle sandwich, and it was while I was eating it, dwelling on the unforgotten insult, that the brilliant idea suddenly occurred to me…

I remembered that the lady was in the habit of going to the pictures regularly on Thursday afternoons. So, at the next opportunity, I nicked off from school one Thursday afternoon, and, purposeful, I walked casually along the narrow alley running beside her long garden's keep-out-the-riff-raff high wall. No-one was about, so I stretched up my arms, leapt, hung, and rapidly monkeyed over the wall.

Stooping low through her shrubs and plants, I reached the conservatory door. It was locked. Luckily, though, there was a handy spade leaning against the wall. Driving the blade into the crack between the door and its frame, I forced it, felt it yield, and I was through into the conservatory. I wondered if the inner door would be locked, too, but it was open, and I stole, cat-footed, into her hall.

The hall had a genteel aura, with its elephant's foot umbrella stand and crystal drops beneath the light bulb. I reached the soft-carpeted staircase, and ascended.

I entered her bedroom. She had a nice collection of clothes in her wardrobe – fur coats, silk Summer dresses, blouses, lacy, embroidered and pearl-buttoned. I reached into the deep pocket of my jacket and pulled forth the tin of treacle I'd bought especially for the occasion with the meagre savings from my piggy bank. Mum's tin of treacle remained innocently in the food safe.

With what gleeful relish I poured the treacle all over those lovely clothes! I made elaborate sweeping figures of eight on those expensive fur coats. I drew squiggly patterns up and down those well-tailored suits, those elegant blouses. Finally, I emptied the rest of the treacle into her underwear drawer, and heaved a sigh of vengeance satisfied.

The task now was to get out unobserved. The alley had been clear when I went in, but was it now? Creep down the stairs, through the reception room, past the piano, the polished rosewood table reflecting my wary face... It was a quiet time of day. Residents were thinking of afternoon tea with dainty triangular sandwiches and Earl Grey infusion. I chanced it, opened the front door, and went confidently down the steps.

I planned many such retaliations in my small bedroom. There always seemed to be someone who had done me wrong, and vindictive was my middle name. I was like my dad in that respect. A mild-mannered man mostly, he too could not stand any form of injustice or slight, and victimisation had him breathing verbal fury. My thoughts were not of the psychopath intent on murdering or injuring severely in any way, but of exacting the levy in the life of any transgressor in the form of an acute unpleasantness.

There lived in our street, in our actual terrace at the refined end, the King Street end, two dear old ladies whom mum had christened 'The Lavender Sisters'. The reason for this label was that both sisters dressed identically in lavender suits of an archaic appearance. Toque hats with white feathers and high-necked buttoned blouses accompanied these suits, as well as black-buttoned shoes with Cuban heels. They seemed an anachronism at the time, when women's skirts were getting much shorter, and even mum wore her sensible tweed skirts just slightly below the knee. They never smiled. That is what I disliked about them most. I think they thought that to smile was somehow *infra dig*. They always wore the same slightly disapproving expressions, and the best another resident of our street could hope for from them was to be deigned acknowledgement with a curt nod. What really irritated me was the way the old 'Lavvy Sisters' (as dad and I called them) upset mum, if, for some reason, they failed to nod in her direction.

"I can't understand it, Sid. I was wearing my best coat to go and visit Clara, and they swept straight past me with their noses in the air."

"Don't let it worry you, Nance, my girl. What do they matter, anyway? They'll probably be dead in about five years' time, and we'll all be dead in a hundred years' time, even the babies along at the fishermen's cottages. Life's too short to worry about dried up old spinsters like them."

"Yes, Sid, but..." She was cut short by a very exaggerated and heavy sigh from dad, letting it be known that he was no longer interested in the conversation and that it was now at an end.

I, though, seethed on behalf of mum. Why did they not acknowledge her? She was decent and respectable. She deserved a nod. Stuck up old cows! How could I get my own back on them on behalf of mum? I sat and thought very deeply in the quietness of my bedroom, and eventually hatched up an elaborate plot...

I had to wait for the right conditions to enact it, though. It needed to be done during the dead of night. It would need to be a dry night, too, when the places I trod would show no impression. And it would need to be done the night before the dustmen were due, when the bins would be nice and full...

Finally, such a night arrived, the conditions aligned perfectly.

I had to wait until three o'clock in the morning to get started on enacting my vengeance. I watched the hands on my birthday-gift watch by the night light in my bedroom. The hours crawled agonisingly by. When three o'clock finally arrived, I silently opened my window and crawled out onto the sill, then, judging carefully the position of the dustbin below, I dropped down into the back garden.

I scaled the dividing walls of the other back gardens until I reached the garden of the 'Lavvy Sisters'. Satisfyingly, their dustbin was crammed to the brim. Now to open their lavatory door. Hopefully there would be a spade in the back garden – most people had spades. If not, I was quite prepared to scoop out the rubbish with my bare hands. But, yes, there was a spade leaning against the wall! Spadefuls of rubbish went into their lavatory bowl, mostly cinders from the coal fire, but also fish heads, potato peelings, stale bread and scraped platefuls of leftover food. The slight noise I made as I carefully scooped up the garbage set my teeth on edge, but finally it was done and I was soon back in my own back garden.

Dad's ladder, just by the lavatory wall, provided the means for my return to my bedroom. I placed it beneath my window, taking care not to scrape and disturb the household. Once in my room, I had to steal downstairs to go back out into the garden to restore the ladder to its usual place. If the lodger awoke and whispered enquiringly, I was off to the lav or I needed a glass of water. Once in the scullery, I unlocked the back door and replaced the ladder. Gone was any trace of my jump descent and scaling return! In again, lock the door, and off back to bed.

It must have been about three weeks later when I happened to be walking along the street and saw the sour old sisters coming towards me. As I passed, I smiled very broadly and sang loudly the beloved song made famous by Charlie Chaplin...

Smile, though your heart is aching,
Smile, even though it's breaking,
You'll find that life is still worthwhile,
If you just smile...

Chapter 7

Confrontations in the Countryside

I believe my father guessed I was behind the dustbin incident, but kept discreetly quiet. My mother, however, thought it right to show some lip-service sympathy for the two old biddies.

"It will be some of those urchins from Marryat Street or Waterloo Street. They roam all hours, up to mischief. I blame the parents. They don't bring them up properly, can't be bothered to find out what they're up to."

"Serve the two old hags right," replied dad. "Thought they weren't in your good books, anyway? Admit it, now. You haven't got much time for them yourself."

"No, but still…" tailed off mum, suppressing a guilty smile.

I was smugly and secretly delighted. I realised happily that I was a chip off the old block. Many times, I had seen dad stand up to the landowners and minor aristocracy that inhabited the countryside when we went off for the day on our frequent walks…

My father loved the countryside with an enthusiastic devotion. Come along each ached-for Sunday, if the early morning was not inclement and the forecast undaunting, we went hiking in Surrey, Kent or Bucks.

Not Essex, though. Dad didn't care for flattish landscape, and deplored the Essex farmers' habit of ploughing up footpaths and leaving the wayfarers' way a raised sodden-ness of muddy furrows and crumbly clarts, murder on the feet.

Up at seven was the rule. Get together the sandwiches of corned beef, cut the previous night, the pile of apples, the Lyons' individual fruit pies, gooseberry or apple purée. No thermos flask – dad preferred to take his small camper's kettle and solid tablet fuel for the tiny lamp, which would set the kettle a-boil in some clearing, sheltered from the wind. An Ordnance Survey map and a bar of Rowntree's Motoring Chocolate completed the accoutrements.

Mum stayed behind. She had accompanied us once, but had lagged back several yards, bemoaning the corns and hard skin on the balls of her big toes, yelling at us to wait, wanting rests every five minutes, and generally making a nuisance of herself. She preferred to stay at home, and that suited us. Dad loved the camaraderie of our two selves taking the sunken tracks which ran about Hascombe and Haslemere and Godalming in his particularly beloved Surrey. We liked our sunken tracks, the studies of light and shade abounding, the enclosed secrecy of our progress through tight tunnels of trees.

One Sunday, we might be off to Amersham and its beech woods. Dad knew all the names of the wild flowers. "See that yellow flower, son? That's lady's bedstraw. That's from the Virgin Mary, an old mediaeval name from when people were more religious. And that little blue flower? That's germander speedwell. And that red one there, that's scarlet pimpernel." So, on we would walk, studying the wild flowers, stroking a young colt's neck, watching a grey squirrel bundle up a tree trunk, marvelling at a dark fairy-ring on grass, or smiling at peculiarly-formed toadstools. We would pause and view a wild flower I hadn't come across before, perhaps the little man-shapes of the green man orchid, the flowers appearing like cut-out shapes of little people hanging down the pithy stem.

What I did not like was the drink we partook of on the way, or rather the attitude of Surrey hostelries' clientele towards an honest working man. When dad came in through a bar door, those fools in their blazers and with their silk scarves tucked about their chins clearly despised the entrant in his cloth cap. They looked down, they shifted aside, viewing the outsider distastefully...

"A pint of draught and a small lemonade," dad asked politely, but my flesh crawled to see the contemptuous glances he drew. I quaked from the door, peering in at the fake old brass and cheerfully pink sporting prints, and the be-ringed barmaids with their elaborate coiffures and accents studiedly classy.

Dad valiantly tangled with snobs whenever the opportunity arose.

Coming along a narrow footpath between thickly overplanted young trees, we were suddenly confronted by a rider on a snorting horse, the animal as surprised to see us as were to view its rolling eyeballs. Atop it sat a young woman tailored for dressage, and her little black cap shadowed beetling brows.

"Get out of my way," she snapped, viciously pulling on the reins for control.

Dad stood his ground. If anything, he seemed to swell out to bar the rider's progress. "I suggest you get out of our way, young woman. This is not a bridle path. It is signposted as a footpath only, and shown as that on my map. You've a bloody cheek to ride down here in the first place, churning up the path with your horse's hooves."

"Stand aside this minute!"

"Not this minute, or this day! We move when you back up. Or if I do move, it'll be to pull you off that animal and rub your face in the mud you've made!"

She somehow turned her horse, and her shrill protests grew muted, as branches whipped back from her vanishing. "People like that!" fumed dad. "They see us as intruders in a county designed for comfortable living in great big houses. Anywhere where there's a few fields and cover, they want foxholes, and they bloody the faces of their emotionless children with the fox's brush. Disgusting practice." Dad hated foxhunting, and often quoted the famous description of it by Oscar Wilde: 'the unspeakable in pursuit of the uneatable'.

On one occasion, he was overjoyed to be asked by hunters whose hounds had lost the scent, "Have you seen the fox?"

"Oh, yes," he had said earnestly, and pointed. "He went in that direction." Which, of course, was exactly the opposite one to the truth.

Countless times, we removed our shoes and socks together to bathe weary feet in a stream. What greater pleasure is there than that bliss of wiggling one's toes while watching the beads of water plink over the run of the stream as it darted and gurgled over washed embedded rocks? Dad would wink at me, and we'd exchange smiles of gentle delight, love flowing between us, as lasting as the running of any stream.

Dad fought with farmers, landowners and householders over disputed rights of way. He would not turn back if a legal right of way existed, not for a king. He argued, told lies, and exaggerated claims to his right to go anywhere. He made sure his maps were up to date to prove his point, in case of challenge.

One such challenge happened near Forest Green. The map showed a path running beside a large, moated house. The guv'nor was lounging in a deckchair when my father clambered over the stile to the immediate left of the drive of the mansion. The way was overgrown, and it looked formidable, but even if there were wire strung across it, it was no matter to dad – he invariably had wire cutters with him.

"And where do you think you are going?" The bloke was up from his deckchair, his face blood-red with fury.

"There's a footpath this way," said dad. "Wants cutting back for hikers."

"There is no footpath. No-one uses it these days. It has lapsed, man."

"Officially? I think not. I am regional organiser for the Ramblers'

Association, and any more bluster from you and I'll have a hundred of our members this way next week with banjos and loud voices and hobnailed boots. We might stray off the path and flatten your petunias. This fine lad here is my son. We're going through."

And go through we did.

In that era, the fields of the Home Counties abounded with four-miles-an-hour processions of parties carrying rucksacks, not to mention the odd portable gramophone churning out Al Bowlly, crooning to girls in serviceable skirts that triangled a foot above rolled down white socks. Each crocodile of cult-folk included at least one bearded pacifist earnestly trying to convert an aggressive companion, and one or two students in dingy macs and pebble glasses, through which they peered longingly at the cheeky swing of the girls' skirts.

The journeys home on the Green Line buses represented for me a sound tuition in the form of good advice. When the wheels were purring through the open countryside, dad used the time on instructing his boy…

"I saw you looking at the legs on that young blonde cyclist. I know you want dates like other boys, but you'll have to watch your step with girls. You will want more than kisses, and that's where caution steps in. If your mates say she's a good thing, ten to one the street bike is what she is, and they'll all have ridden her. Watch out. She could give you a dose of the coachman's." I knew my rhyming slang: coachman's box = pox. "Remember this, though, son: true love goes far beyond physical attraction. When the right girl comes along, you'll be sick at heart wanting her for more than her body. It won't be a feeling like anything else."

When we got home, mum was always pleased to see us, and we'd have roast beef and Yorkshire pudding, done to a turn. She'd have made a roly-poly currant pudding, done in a cloth. "Have some more, there's plenty. Cup of tea? You must be tired. Want a bowl of warm water to soak your feet in, son?"

We knew that if she had come with us there would not be the cooked meal and cosy reception to come home to. We feared that one day she may forget her previous discomfort on the walks and want to come with us. If she ever tentatively suggested that she may want to join us next time, dad would have his excuses ready. "Good job you weren't with us today. The stepping stones at Burford were slimy, and you might have slipped. And to crown it all, we were chased by cows." Mum shuddered. She had had a lucky escape. She was afraid of cows.

Dad was always ready with a scheme to put mum off. Once, he soaked our remnant sandwiches in a stream to prove what a downpour we had been through. "Soaked right through the rucksack. Feel my jacket." He'd deliberately dampened that. Or, as a trencherman's meal proceeded, dad inserted, through mouthfuls of grub, some remark outlining not a good day out at all. "Nice to sit in warmth and comfort. Had to get up sharpish when we sat down for our lunch. Red ants running about all over the place!"

Chapter 8

Destined for Better Things

Mum and dad were determined to rear a genius.

As soon as my fourth birthday had passed, I was sat firmly at the kitchen table for longer and longer periods of time with comics and 'The Cat Sat on the Mat' picture storybooks thrust under my nose. After checking to see that I was fully awake, reading instruction began. The ABC, the sounds the letters made … it was quite a competent time of tuition. The boy had to be able to read before he went to school. And read he did. There were no muttered curses or exasperated sighs should I stumble over a word. Mum taught with patience at her elbow and encouragement on her lips. That I was avid to learn was taken for granted.

It got so that I squirmed when relations called. "He can do this, he can do that, he's spelling incredibly well for his age already." I upset the revolting Uncle Ned by relieving him of a sixpence (untold riches), promised should I be able to rattle off correctly the letters of the hugely impossible word 'reconciliation'.

Needless to say, when I made the acquaintance of my first classmates, they met up with an odiously big-headed brat. In a few days at my junior school, I had won the creaky heart of Miss Cooper, the apple-cheeked English teacher, with my ability to win disgracefully regularly the whole one penny reward she bestowed upon the best speller of the day. I fully deserved the furious looks I received from the ill-clad dockland wretches confined behind our one-piece bench-and-sloping-desk contraptions. I looked down on their scruffy hand-me-down clothes, their ragged plimsolls and their tousled hair. I knew how they lived: three in a bed; bread and jam for Sunday tea (lard on the bread, if they were lucky); not a snot-rag between the lot of them, and I with a clean hanky daily in my top jacket pocket. Not for me the charitable gesture, the benevolent eye on those less fortunate. I had a lot to learn. In time, they taught me a little humility, but it was one boy in particular, Lenny, who taught me compassion.

Lenny was a boy with a jacket several sizes too big for him, rubbed-grey flannel short trousers, and long grey socks that sagged round his ankles. He had a permanently snotty nose, and often looked tired, with sad, lacklustre eyes. Having several siblings younger than himself, he had to share his bed with Cedric, a younger brother who guaranteed him sleepless nights. "Our Ced didn't half kick last night," he would say with a sigh, before settling down conscientiously to do his work that day.

Lenny tried. He really did try. He listened avidly to the teacher, patiently scrawled his essays, and frowned hard to answer the mental arithmetic questions hurled from the lips of Dinger Bell.

Mr. Bell, 'Dinger', as he was known, was leonine in appearance, with a thick head of grey hair and a lean body, which he swung between the desks in a prowling lope, bunch of keys in hand. His key chain held a multitude of keys of all shapes and sizes, and made a formidable weapon. Woe betide any boy not paying attention.

"Tinsley! Three half-crowns, two florins and a sixpence. What do they make? Come on, what do they make?" And if the answer was slow in coming, Dinger's hand lifted, the keys were swung, and instead of a quick slap over and done with, one was dented on the nut in a number of painful places simultaneously. I am sure certain pits and dells on my cranium result from that tyrant's attention.

Lenny was not good at arithmetic. And Dinger let the whole class know it.

"You! Smith! Yes, you, Leonard Smith! This is your exercise book!" He held it up for us all to mock. "Wrong, wrong and wrong! The same story, right down to the bottom of the page. When I see your book, I automatically prepare to make huge red crosses. You are a dolt, Smith. What are you?"

"A dolt, sir," said Lenny meekly.

This humiliation was not punishment enough. The condemnation would be followed by a mighty swipe with the bunch of keys onto the back of Lenny's head. Even I, prig that I was, felt sorry for Lenny.

But then came the memorable day, the day that will go down in the history of the school, when Lenny had had enough...

The day started like any other, except perhaps that Lenny looked a little more tired than usual. We all sat at our desks, ready to commence writing whatever essay Miss Cooper chose to set us, only to find that

Miss Cooper was not in attendance, and that Dinger Bell would be taking her place. The essay he set for us – 'My Pet'.

We all dutifully opened our exercise books, took up our pens and began writing. Each of us had one of these pens, issued by the school, nib included, as well as accompanying blotting paper. The pens were filled from inkwells in the desks, which were periodically topped up from large pottery jars by responsible monitors. Convenient felt tips and biros were not in evidence in my early years.

Lenny, though, did not commence writing. Instead, he raised his hand. "Please, sir. I haven't got a pet."

"No," replied Dinger, ominously. "I don't suppose you would have. Well pretend, idiot! Make one up!"

Lenny put his pen in the inkwell, but did not notice the glob of blotting paper he had pulled from the inky depths. It fell onto his book, forming a messy blot.

"Fool! Idiot! Clumsy, messy wretch!" The keys swung, but Lenny jumped up, knocking them from the outraged master's hand. He followed this with a punch to the nose of Dinger Bell, which was amazing in its power from such an undernourished ten-year-old.

The roar which issued from the throat of Mr. Bell could probably have been heard in Hammersmith Broadway. It brought the headmaster hurrying from his study. "Mr. Bell, whatever has happened?"

Dinger Bell, clutching his nose, could only gasp, "This boy ... this boy..."

We were all, I feel sure, absolutely terrified, petrified that we, too, would somehow be drawn into the looming punishment. Terrified for Lenny, too, and, smugness forgotten, I felt desperately sorry for him.

We heard the loud thwacks from the headmaster's study.

Thwack! Thwack! Thwack! Thwack! Thwack! Thwack!

Six of the best. Then...

Thwack!

Another one?

Thwack!

Not eight!?

Thwack!

Nine!? Little Cissie Bartlett, usually such a chirpy little girl, put her head down on the desk and started to cry. The headmaster had left the door of his study open for us all to hear.

Thwack!

Ten! Lenny was sobbing and wailing, but his ordeal was finally at an end. The headmaster had probably tired himself out, and ten was his limit.

Lenny did not come back into the classroom. He did not come back into the school. He was expelled on the spot and sent home. What kind of reception he would get there, I dreaded to think. He would probably receive another cuffing from his parents. I knew that it was no good complaining to my mum and dad if I had been punished at school. Adults sided with adults in those days, and children were considered to have a propensity for naughtiness and needed to be curbed. I would like to think that Lenny's was a rags-to-riches story, and that he would rise above his background and become successful. I wanted him to be happy, but I doubted he would be. For a while, I wondered what had happened to him, but this soon passed. I had other things to think about.

The caning of Lenny did not really surprise me. I had already summed up the headmaster as a martinet who liked wielding the whippy cane, bringing it to palm or buttocks with a glee which showed in his eyes while he kept his mouth straight. He was only interested in boys with brains and promise. The rest of the kids were cattle, who came each day to the sound of the handbell rung for lessons as cows return to the shed for milking.

Later on, the sheep were separated from the goats. With several others, I found myself twice-weekly in the headmaster's study for extra tuition, with a view to passing the frightfully difficult papers in the Junior County Scholarship exam. If I won through brilliantly, I could anticipate a classy uniform and attendance at Upper Latymer, where they had things like prefects and a rowing club and masters with impressive degrees. There, the boys wore worried looks, since their parents were constantly fighting hunger in order to pay for the uniform and extras recommended. Failure to do so was not tolerated. "You are subtly informed, dear Sir or Madam, that it is despicable not to undertake the extras expected. Close the door as you leave."

At the Junior School, there was a very great awareness of your place in life. In morning assembly, the hymn often selected for the day would be 'All Things Bright and Beautiful', with its one particularly odious verse, written to discourage any aspirations to social advancement. That particular verse seemed always to be sung louder by the assembled staff on the raised dais, as they looked down on their pupils in more ways than one. 'Know your place, riff-raff,' it implied...

The rich man in his castle
The poor man at his gate
God made them high or lowly
And ordered their estate

However, the headmaster did want us to succeed in the coming exam; the more pupils that passed, the more prestigious for him. There was no altruism in his wish for us to better ourselves.

The headmaster's study was the holy of holies. There persisted here an invisible blanket of righteousness, correct behaviour and rectitude. Each aspiring scholarship boy was interviewed, one by one.

I was called to the presence, and stood before the desk, with its green leather covering and tooled edge. On the wall behind was a faded print of 'And When Did You Last See Your Father?', the little Royalist boy in his silken suit and with golden curls stood in all his childish innocence before the stern Cromwellian interrogator. I stood before the headmaster, secretly loathing him.

"Now, Tinsley, are you serious about wanting to pass this exam?"

"Yes, sir."

"And are you prepared to work hard?"

"Yes, sir."

I understand that you are not very good at mathematics. Your arithmetic seems to me satisfactory, but you struggle on algebra and geometry, do you not?"

"Yes, sir." I certainly struggled on algebra. I saw no point in it. I was too young for such esoteric rubbish. Would I go into a shop for apples at two a penny and work out the cost by the 'if y equals, or let x equal wotsit' method? Not bloody likely!

Dad bribed me. He said to forget Upper Latymer (he wasn't intending to fork out for their extras). But if I passed for West Kensington Central, he would buy me (well, at least put down a deposit on) a Raleigh Dawn Safety Model bicycle with dynamo lights, raised handlebars, Brooks saddle, and large black saddlebag.

I passed for West Ken Central Boys' School, scraping through the maths paper with barely a pass mark and probably thanks to the examiner having been in a good mood. So, dad presented me with the bicycle and the little payment book for taking to Hood's the bike shop. He'd forked out a whole pound. I had the balance to pay at half-a-crown a week.

"How will I manage to pay it off, dad?"

His advice? Get a paper round.

The paper round was a bit of an education. All the paper boys were exploited at the local newsagents, earning only a few bob a week, not only for delivering the papers at the crack of dawn, but also for having to go round our routes on Friday evenings to collect the cash from the customers, who, in some cases, were loath to pay up. A typical response might be:

"The papers? I'm out of collar, out of work. Here's two bob off the six weeks' arrears. Go on, note it down, you pestering little bastard. And how come we haven't had no *Home Chat* this week?"

"The boss said no magazines till you're straight."

"The tight git! He wants castrating! Not that that would worry him, with that frump of a wife of his!"

Even more typical was:

"I paid for years when I was in plenty, so tell him he'll have to carry me for a bit longer till I find a job." Often, this was said whilst a Woodbine was being pulled from a packet of twenty, and whilst beer breath from the pub wafted out over me. There were some, it seemed, who had a system of priorities when it came to paying for necessities.

Chapter 9

Scholarship Boy

Mum lost no time in letting everyone know that her clever son had passed to go to West Kensington Central Boys' School.

The adults murmured polite congratulations, but I had lost any street cred I ever had with the other kids in the street. At this time, I was now striving desperately to court popularity with the bigger lads in Angel: I took scads of comics out into the street, threw the bundle wildly skywards, shouting, "Scrambles!" – an invitation for fast acquisition; I bought sweets and handed them round, pear drops, liquorice allsorts, coconut macaroons, all manner of goodies. They accepted all of these gifts, but rejected me.

"Who's a little posh kid now? Off to West Ken, are we? Horrible little snot."

"I ain't a posh kid, I ain't, I ain't!" I protested, in the broadest Cockney I could muster.

All to no avail, of course. And when I returned dejectedly to the house, sans comics and sweets, mum would make sure there were lots of little chats about what I was going to be, giving me a glimpse of what lurked ahead for me, an awfully sober future where I would wear a stiff collar and check my fingernails each morning for grime before setting out for 'The Office'. This imaginary future workplace appeared to loom in her mind as some shining edifice built of pink marble and beaten gold, where genteel typists and gentlemanly clerks bestowed sweet smiles of welcome on the newcomer who had come to join their ranks.

Kitted out in my new uniform (but still with short trousers), I entered the superior educational establishment of West Ken. It was a revelation to me. Most masters actually treated us with respect, and, unbelievably, I found many of the lessons actually interesting.

My favourite master was Stumpy Moore, a lovely man who I believe had suffered some sort of wound in the First World War which made him limp, hence his nickname. On Friday afternoons he took us for English, and he made these afternoons golden. Suddenly putting down an instructive set book, he would say, "Anyone fancy listening to a rattling fine tale instead?" From Stumpy's readings, I entered the worlds of Edgar Wallace and Edgar Allan Poe – he favoured spy stories and tales of things which went bump in the night. He wore heavy tweed suits of mustard, ginger and green, dull and lifeless, but his personality was warm. He loved all children. He encouraged the bright, but more importantly never made a struggling scholar feel he was not keeping up with rest of the class. Nice man.

After a year at West Ken, I took stock of my progress. I was viewed with suspicion by the more circumspect masters – they considered me a comic, a clever-clogs, a potential time bomb in classes, with my way of finding fun in a serious subject...

"There are three types of clause," Pop Norton had intoned pompously in one of his dull English Grammar lessons.

"Three types of clause," I muttered aside for those near. "Cat's claws, dog's claws and Santa Claus." Of course, Pop heard me and I got scowled at and given lines to do, which was the superior way of discipline at West Ken. 'Don't cane the boy – that will be over and done with. Give him an imposition. Make him write 'Manners maketh man' or 'I must learn not to be impertinent' two hundred times.' And they always knew if you had aligned three pens in rubber bands to scrawl three lines at a time.

My aversion was Mr. Dupenchal, who had a face like a particularly aggressive bloodhound. He taught Mathematics, including ghastly algebra and loathsome trigonometry, both of which were of no use or sense to me. I was going to be neither a surveyor nor an architect, and was totally incapable of understanding what a cosine or a tangent was. I would never recognise a cosine from a coal mine, or a tangent from a tangerine. That was the extent of my unfathoming attendance at Dupenchal's repellent classes.

"Your exercise book, Tinsley. Full of mistakes!" He held the offending book between finger and thumb, and continued, "Your brains must be non-existent. I could well do without you!"

How fervently I wished that could be – no Maths any day of the week! I preferred Science, with its spacious classrooms, fascinating glass tubes, Bunsen burners and chemical mixture experiments, and English, where I'd find magical new ways of expressing myself in composition, and learn about similes and metaphors and the wonders of poetry, like assonance and alliteration.

If Maths was a bugbear, P.T. was even worse. I steadfastly refused to soar over the vaulting horse with legs astride. I adamantly refused, fearing crushed bollocks, envisaging only making it halfway over and ending up straddling the horse, whacking and bruising my vulnerable appendages. So, I did not launch – would not, despite threats and coaxing. Instead, I condescended to scrambling over, but that was all.

"Do ten backward rolls on the mat for refusing!" And the sharp coir bristles dug into my neck, as if mum had taken a stiff broom to me in disgust for non-co-operation.

What is this madness of the English for strain and stress in the name of healthy exercise? All my school life, I was to protest at violent onslaughts programmed for my muscles. I would have none of it.

There was a certain master who, on one occasion, determined to get me participating in the annual sports day, insisted on entering my name for the hundred yards sprint.

"No, sir," I countered. "I'll attend, but I'm taking no part. Not in any event. You can't make me."

He took on colour and approached my desk. "You will do as I say, young skiver!" Thrusting his face closer to mine, he said, "I shall personally see to it that you are at the tape in running shorts and plimsolls."

On the day, he stood at the side-line. The entrants for the sprint lined up, some of the energetic fools limbering up, doing a sort of knee joint release, or running on the spot. Tinsley waited, aloof, at the head of his lane. The starter pointed his silly little pistol to the sky and fired, and off it went, *bang* (or rather a dampish *phut*), to herald the start of this puerile pastime.

The runners sped off, flying for the dimly seen finishing rope. I still stood there at the starting line, and, when the others had reached their goal, I strolled over unhurriedly to the bewildered master who had got me there. "What? How..." he spluttered, scarcely able to speak.

"Well, sir," I said, "you have seen me at the tape in running shorts and plimsolls. But I didn't say I'd run, did I?"

"You unsportsmanlike wretch!"

"Unathletic, sir. If I run, I get awfully out of breath and a stitch in my side. Not built for athletics, me, sir."

The headmaster didn't get involved. He was only ever involved in dire misdemeanours. The outraged sports master merely sent a letter home to my parents, but for once my parents sided with me.

"Sport won't get you a good job in an office," observed mum.

"Muddied oafs and flannelled fools, that's what sportsmen are," Dad stated emphatically.

Shortly after this incident, there occurred a remarkable concession from the headmaster that I hoped may have sprung from my refusal to participate in sport.

After the customary hymns and Bible reading at morning assembly, the headmaster stood by the lectern. "I am aware that there are those boys for whom physical activity may not be advisable. Therefore, on sports day afternoons, those boys not wishing to participate may instead attend a concert at Westminster Hall, and may put their names forward for this concession."

I could hardly believe my ears. My admiration for this most enlightened of headmasters soared.

How I enjoyed those concerts! We listened to the exciting and thunderous *Ride of the Valkyries* by Wagner, thrilled to the pathos of the Max Bruch violin concerto... I listened, enthralled.

Once, there was a piano recital dedicated to the works of Frederic Chopin. I went home full of enthusiasm for such beautiful music.

"Well," said dad, "if you like that sort of music so much, why don't we go to Shepherd's Bush Market and look through the second hand records for classical music?"

Thus began a quest for finding as many classical records as possible: *Liebestraum* by Franz Liszt; Chopin preludes; the overture from *Tannhäuser* by my particular favourite, Wagner. So it was that Sunday afternoons in the front room were filled with the melodies of the great composers, and I can owe my love of classical music to the understanding of my headmaster, and, of course, to my lovely and ever supporting old dad.

Chapter 10

Hobbies and Interests

29 Angel was a hive of activity in the evenings.

Dad thoroughly enjoyed scowling at the radio whenever Harry Hemsley imitated his appallingly squeaky trio of odious nippers, Elsie, Winnie and Johnny. "Comic, he calls himself? The cat's funnier than him. That last crack he pinched from Elsie and Doris Waters, you mark my words."

Mum invariably darned, but listened to us, not the wireless, for dad always used the opportunity to employ a subtle form of questioning on me regarding my doings at school while he'd been at work during the week. I think he felt, "I've had a rough day at work today painting buses, but that son of mine has likely just been doing easy sums or getting a penny for spelling well."

"Football you had, today," he'd say. "Wormwood Scrubs playing fields. You skive out of it, as per usual?"

I squirmed, anti-athletic. "The train: I dozed off and got carried on a couple of stations. Then, when I reached the Scrubs, the second half was on. I was put in goal."

"Let many in?"

"Fourteen!"

Dad sighed. He felt he had to ask, but had no interest in sport.

Later, we heaved out a virgin jigsaw puzzle, a Lumar one from Woolworth's. It might be lupins and foxgloves in an English country garden, a Moorish archway before a souq, or maybe a giant steamship, or a loco belching steam.

Speaking of engines, sometimes we took an oil heater upstairs and played trains in my room. In a fit of expending madness, dad had, one Christmas, bought me a real scale-model steam train. Bassett-Lowke were the makers. The whole ensemble of the engine and tender gleamed black with scarlet lines, and while I think the engine's name was *King George V*, I would not take money on it. I only knew that dad enjoyed trains more than I, if that were possible. In a frenzy of removal, everything went from my room, chucked out none too gently, and down went the lines, an ellipse. It was stoutly constructed, as were the train's many trucks, made wholly of steel and wood, the couplings in no way flimsy, the wheels heavy, the buffers solidly fixed. How dad grovelled about the boiler when it got up steam! Meths in the burner caused blue flames to flicker, the thin vapour soon became a head of warm steam, and the engine was off along the track.

We might be up there for hours. Then mum would wail up, "What about preparing the fire for tomorrow, Sid? I want wood chopped. And you forgot to mend my ironing board leg, and you did promise."

"Women!" dad would fume. "Always something. 'Do this, do that...' I suppose I'll have to go down."

While he was away, I'd watch the lovely puffer whizz round, and rejoice. Dad tended to hog the action. While I avidly watched the engine, I would hear him outside, wielding the chopper in the murk of the garden, the candle he was working by flitting out far too often and wanting continual relighting. I would hear him cursing whenever careless handling gave him a splinter in a finger already scarred where paint flakes had penetrated or sharp metal had scraped.

Dad's hands were a sight, for all their competence, but I loved to see him make things. Often, I helped with home carpentry...

Whenever dad pulled out his toolbox and went for the wood he had brought home for a job, I worried about the end product. Trouble was, mum was so grudging with her praise of an article built cleverly and undoubtedly deserving of admiration. It was as if dad was not worthy of praise. He must not only be subordinate, but constantly be reminded of his status of second-best; her first love had been a swaggering young soldier from the Dominions. I had seen his photo in her gold locket, she a young lovely with swan neck and glossy black hair in a bun, he fair-haired with pale eyes the colour of which I could not tell from the sepia-tinted photograph.

Dad would throw down the implement he had been using, an adze, a bradawl, a hammer, and as it landed with a loud thump on the floor he would storm, "Why do I bother? A walking wage packet, that's me. Come in from work, 'Here's your dinner, Sid, don't say too much.'"

I thought of the day I had first seen that locket on her dressing table and guilty curiosity had caused me to open it. The locket opened into two bivalve divisions revealing the photographs, reminding her of the lost love still deep in her heart. I look at his smiling face, a persuader, full of charm. I assume that without knowing anything about him. I hate the boy who came over and conquered, preceding dad in my mother's affections. He with a kitbag was nothing but a shitbag. 'She has a second choice for a husband, has mum,' I thought. How that rankled! And how aware I was of dad sharing my bitter knowledge. He wouldn't have stood a chance if his predecessor had gone down on one knee instead of hurrying up the gangplank on his way back to Australia.

There was a time when dad thought he would try to make me as skilled a craftsman as himself. Vain hope! Fishing out his monogrammed toolbox, he painstakingly, and with much elaborate explanation, told me what each tool did and how to use it.

"See this here, son? This is a spokeshave."

"Thought he wrote *The Merchant of Venice*."

"Clever twerp. Where are you going?"

"Outside. I want to use a tool of my own for a necessary job in the khazi. It's all that tea."

"This hammer," dad would insist, "isn't just a hammer. See that blunt end?"

"What's it for?" I responded. That pleased him.

He gently smote the back of my neck. "It's for hammering a useless git. I'm wasting my time. We'll do what you want. Indulge that sweet tooth of yours."

So, we turned mum out of the scullery and either made peppermint creams, lavender creams, or a particularly sticky and tough kind of treacle toffee consisting of demerara sugar and butter, with perhaps a few cornflakes thrown in as the toffee set to give it a more inventive appearance. Sometimes dad tried out a new curry recipe, a strange sauce to pour over boiled cod on the supper menu, but usually for the next couple of days every bottom and top set of jaws ached from stick-jaw mastication. Mum liked the treacle toffee, too.

Anything was liable to happen in 29 Angel in the line of eccentric behaviour, so much so that mum took no notice when the old man had a fit for what she called 'a daft half hour'.

He'd look from the side of a hardbound library book, a William Le Queux or Russell Thorndike gripper, a manic gleam in his eye. "Gold dust," he'd say. "Get the cocoa. I know there's Marie biscuits in the food safe – a whole packetful."

Manually, he crushed the biscuits to dust on a sheet of newspaper. He stirred in the cocoa and liberally sprinkled in sugar crystals, finally crunching it all together in a mound. We were supposed to not only eat the resultant aridly dry concoction, but enjoy it, as well. I didn't want to be a wet blanket and curb his enthusiasm, but I did not have as much liking for the mixture of biscuit crumbs and Tate & Lyle as he obviously did. Afterwards, my mouth always felt like the floor of a sanded birdcage. And there was so much of it to get through!

Strangely, though, mum seemed to enjoy it, eating her way through her large portion with seeming relish.

Or, dad might suddenly exclaim, "Oxford and Cambridge!" A stranger wouldn't glimmer what was about to happen. It meant I had to spring to my feet and drop down full-length onto the mat in front of the fire with long legs outstretched. Dad did the same, and positioned himself with the soles of his shoes touching mine. I grasped his upper arms, he interlaced mine. Then, alternately, one bent the knees and went slack bodied while the other member of the 'crew' stiffened his legs and heaved. Up I'd go, then him, then me... This went on until the boat reached the harbour, and only dad was allowed to end or cancel the trip.

When dad had found a library book disappointing, or when he wasn't in the mood for any of the aforementioned pursuits, to relieve his ennui there would be a wine tasting session. Dad made literally gallons of home-made wine. A large china jug and bowl set adorned with blue transfer prints of Arabs riding camels, it received, frothing and steamy, whatever came off the gas after a long hard boil, with all of us breathing in the sometimes fruity, more often floral, incense wafted up from the gas cooker in the scullery. Wine could be extracted from banana, beetroot, sugar beet, bramble, cowslip and oak leaf, separately, I hasten to add. We had wine from gorse, oranges, apples, plums, rice, corn ears, tufts of barley... Wine from pea pods, potatoes, parsnip, white clover, cloves, elderflowers, elderberries... Add yeast. That was in the line of 'light the blue touch paper and retire immediately', in my opinion. What had once been innocuous would soon be raving in the bowl, seething, producing a frantic ferment of desirable alcohol.

There were cupboards full of bottled wine everywhere in the house. All the bottles bore dated labels, so the old man's eyes could gleam in reading that this specimen, black cherry, just like a mature liqueur, was all of a year old, and then some. "Fish it out. Now grab a bottle of rhubarb. Hey, what's this? Goosegog? We'll try it. And we may as well see how the maturing apricot is getting along, as well."

We started off interestedly sober, then went through the stage of murmuring comment, on to reeling praise, and finally to lolling, incoherent appreciation. Mum was laughing at a poor joke of dad's, years old. He looked my way, slightly ashamed, when she reached out and squeezed his leg, high up.

My eyes couldn't focus straight. The walls were on the shift, dancing in a kind of haze. "What was that one, dad?"

"Gawd knows, and he won't split." He poured out more parsnip with a loud guffaw, sounding like a moose with a hacking sore throat. "Drink up! What about this golden bottle, straight from the cornfield?"

Every so often of an evening, there came a modestly quiet knock, so muted we could not be sure anyone had lifted the heavy black hoop over the fat boss on the stout front door. Whoever checked out the suspected caller found dad's rather self-effacing mate, Percy, bald and hesitant, before the whitened door step.

"Hello," Perce would breathe, just about audible. Perce was Scots, and was savagely henpecked by a waspish wife and demanding uppish daughter of whom 'THINGS WERE EXPECTED'. Perce worked as a booking clerk on the railway, and himself ran on extremely straight lines of behaviour owing to a religious household upbringing. Percy swore not at all, and the foul weed tobacco was not for him, so it was a source of puzzlement for me how his daughter had arrived in such an abstinent life. But Perce drank when persuaded. And how my dad could persuade, in a gentle wheedle… "There's a little mature parsnip you haven't tried, old cock." Percy winced at the endearment, but nodded acceptance, cheered up visibly. The poor sod didn't get the chance to smile much. I had seen his missus. Straight line lips, face like a county court summons. I had seen and admired his daughter from afar, the other side of a busy road. Introduced to her later, she looked me up and down as if inspecting a lavatory chain for germs.

A routine persisted. Dad brought forth bottles of all shapes and colours. Fat bottles, thin bottles, small, large, pink, orange, fawn, clear, ruby, purple, all glowing temptingly under Percy's thin eager nose. Like a conjuror producing objects to amaze his audience, dad offered shot glass after shot glass of 'samples'. Sampling, Percy invariably had a chaser of the same, began talking for once, and actually cracked a harmless and rather unfunny joke or two. Then, having reached a certain stage, that of maudlin admissions of his subordinate role in his rigid household, he soon put his shiny head on the table, scalp uppermost.

"It was that dandelion brew done it this time." Dad went for his trilby. "I'll have to get this lump on to a bus, somehow."

"Lurch him all the way home," said mum. "Otherwise that spiteful wife of his will be here to complain, and I don't want her gimlet eyes contemplating my kitchen with open contempt."

One evening, Perce went too far. He had had glass after glass of his favoured corn wine, a clear and innocuous looking liquid which went down like white fire. The old man was talking to him about wireless circuits, an interest shared. Perce lost count of the shots he had gulped.

That happy in his cups, he had surely not known such a glow of late. He went on drinking. Perhaps he had discovered a misty Utopia in his swirling thoughts and wanted to stay there. The fact that his wife and daughter were visiting relatives in Bonnie Scotland could have been responsible for his rash imbibing, with naught to fear when he reeled back home. At last he rose and, as suddenly, collapsed in a heap. All the dignity of the soberly dressed family man was gone in a limpness of legs unsupportive. One arm slid from the top of the table, inadequately clutched to prevent him from sinking.

"Bloody hell!" Dad smoothed the stubble on his chin. "This is a right bricklayer's hod of a situation. I can't lift that!"

Mum was amused. "How fortunate that Edna won't view the inebriated. That's the word she would have flung into his face, if at home. Only one thing for it, Sid. Go to the Broadway rank for a taxi. You can haul him into the back of the taxi with the taxi man to help."

So, dad saw Perce to his council house in posh Barnes with the aid of the taxi man, that geezer relieved that at least there was no spew on his leather seats.

We were told in due course that Perce awoke in his rumpled bed, bursting for a slash. He jumped up, shaved carefully, and went to work with a dry tongue and head buzzing. When he arrived at the booking office, he announced, "I'm not late, but I thought I would be the way I feel."

"No, you're not late," said his colleague in the booth. "But Perce, where were you yesterday?"

Percy had had too much of my father's potent hospitality, and had slept the clock round.

Chapter 11

Our Back Garden: Portal to Paradise

I spent long happy hours in the back garden, a space no more than a hop, skip and jump wide by eighteen strides down. It became, for me, a playground adored. There was so much to see and do there. In my mind's eye, I am back in that haven with its urban flora and fauna...

Squatting and now and then jumping crabwise, I proceed along a border of pint milk bottles embedded reversed in the earth, and I peer at dark green ferns seen opaquely through the moisture-misted glass. I can raise a most unmusical score of tinkles from the bottles with a spoon. If I turn about and maintain my crouch, I can just about reach the patch of nasturtiums which sometimes provide a change on the menu for me, the large thin leaves placed between bread, making a tickle-nose peppery sandwich.

On washing days, dad's long johns hang like the truncated and bloodless corpse of a felon executed upside down. It amuses me to pat the seat of the pants to give the woolly wretch a swing. Further down the line, the bedraggled skeining of several pairs of mum's stockings are there for me to pull down. Stretching them until the tautness of the line strains at my fingers, I let go, and the stockings do a springy, limp dance, amazingly abandoned, considering who they belong to.

I wander, and watch the spiders, large and small, lurking motionless atop their web retreats. The sucked husk of an emerald-bodied fly must surely advertise what a voracious monster one particular bulbous creature is, with his sinister white trace markings, very like a malformed cross. I amble on to search for Joey the toad, who likes to hole up in crevices low to the ground. I circumnavigate Cuthbert, our tortoise, stiffly stumbling off nowhere, with his shell tilting to awkward angles as he rocks over uneven ground.

Near Old Man Warner's wall, I pause to renew the pleasure of riding on a remnant toy from infant days. My rocky horse is more dapple grey than ever now, soaked by rain and blistered by Summer days, which have warmed his scoop-hollow saddle for urging-on buttocks. His pink-painted mouth has peeled away, revealing the hard wood beneath.

Michaelmas daisies, goldenrod and marigolds straggle weedily in the flowerbed running parallel to Mrs. Price's back garden. She has a massive mangle in her back garden, and I like to watch the cascades of water pouring out from her sheets as she feeds them through the rollers on a Monday.

The T junction flowerbed end of the garden would not have disgraced the Chelsea Flower Show. There rose, splendiferous and enviable, dad's prize double dahlias, flame flowers and lemon loveliness marching in petalled profusion before a rambling prickliness of a blackberry bush, cultivated with loving care. The bush's fruit burgeon heavily, drooping in succulent clusters, the berries that big and soft, that eager, gathering soon had juice running under the sleeves of jumper or pullover and hands stained a royal purple. The fruit provides fillings for numerous pies. Together with sliced apple, snowdrifts of sugar, and one or two cloves, we had afters fit for a king.

Before the dahlias rose a Chinese box kite on a creosoted telephone pole; Dad's awesomely tall dipole aerial, a threat to low-flying aircraft, swayed alarmingly in strong winds, and made mum mutter resentment every time she had to adjust the washing line through the pulley, as the aerial stuck up in front of the clothes pole. She hated the smell of the creosote when it was applied, too. "Mind my line pole," she came out and yelled. "That gassy stink! You wielding that brush, anointing your ridiculous aerial! Anyone would think this was Broadcasting House! And what do we get, with you twiddling knobs and oscillating for hours? Moscow, apparently, but all I ever hear is a mumble and crackle with some foreigner burbling gibberish!"

My father frequently groused about the beds behind the bottle border showing depressions all over the place, as these made the few plants striving to survive there either sit on the brow of a minor hillock or nestle in a sunken dark dell. This was due to my giving way to sudden urges to have a dig. What I expected to find in this one small strip of land remains a mystery. I sifted excavated mixtures of soil, clay and gravel with the avidity of an archaeologist hunting for Inca burial relics, but all I came across was the dry orange leg bone of a cat, perished without even a ring of white stones to mark its resting place, the shards of some cheap crockery, which when rubbed clean revealed a transfer print of blue roses, and some bits of iridescent glass. Well, that's not entirely true; there was also the discovery of a threepenny bit, a lead soldier with the paint worn off, and, once, a well-constructed German model of a touring car, its back seats packed with mud. Each of those discoveries made my day.

"We don't want you growing up to be a navvy," mum cautioned. "We haven't coaxed you through to a scholarship place in West Ken Central for you to spit on your hands in a trench running with sewer water. We have plans for you, Stanley, you should know that. You will sit in an office and wear white collars, I hope."

In those days, did I secretly long for the simple untrammelled life of a labourer in outside employment, with no more responsibility than to complete a hole dug this deep from there to here? I could not know that one day I would climb in the Civil Service with outward pristine appearance, while my soul rotted within me, and my brooding thoughts dwelt on the uninspiring grind of dealing with dull forms instead of the richness of life in God-given fresh air. As I wielded my little trowel and scooped out a serpentining centipede (which had me recoiling), with the sun on my back, and savouring the dank, delightful smell of green things growing, why didn't I then resolve that they could push all they liked but I would rather have a job where I'd be 'Stan, mate' and not 'Stanley the clerk' at the desk where the shadow falls?

At the opposite end from the garden wall was the crunchy mound of a pile of coke. I could climb up and play 'King of the Castle' there, but had to be careful not to start an avalanche that would scatter chunks all over the flagstones, causing mum to say, "Must you? There'll be dust in your earholes and down your socks, and shoes cost money. Get your plimsolls on at once! Scholarship boy! More like a madman let out for the day!"

Going into the garden presented many hazards: I'd curse if I slid in the soggy splodge of cake crumb and bread crusts put out for the birds; I'd have to pick my way carefully to avoid Cuthbert, ambling aimlessly, or Joey, sat there with his bellows-bag of a throat working and toad eyes boggling; and I'd swear out loud if one of the sheets flapping on the clothes line billowed out to cling to my face in a damp embrace, like a ghost from a watery grave. On Summer days, one ran into the green haze of greenfly. Wasps dipped and swooped like angry flying humbugs, far from sweet. I had to watch out for snails' silver trails – I'd be upset all day if I trod disastrously and made one look like a stray whelk off a fish stall. There was a snakes-and-ladders avoidance puzzle of creatures on the flagstones: step over that crack so as not to squash a black slug in its wet liquorice cling; retreat when this hard-cased stag beetle scuttles into danger; make a wide stride for the family of woodlice coming out from under this pebble I've kicked out of the gravel. Even in the lav I wasn't out of trouble. There'd be another kind of spider stranded on the glaze of the pan. I'd run back indoors for the lifeline of a paper spill that the fool can climb to safety on.

There was fun to be had from taking food into the garden for the birds, though, watching the pecking order form as they flocked; the ring of scruffy sparrows wary; the starlings bullying and chasing and selecting the bigger breadcrumbs; the pretty blue and saffron timidity of the finches, patient on the fringe, waiting for the leavings; the beating visitation of death-wings, as a raven flew in from the distant church.

Near Old Man Warner's wall, dad had ambitiously planted a sunflower. What a carry on we had when I had to stand on a chair and, two-handed, hold the tall stem, while dad changed over the next in a succession of longer and longer stakes. The huge, top-heavy flower broke out at the top of the stem with all the pride of a Labour Party candidate's rosette when he's voted in after a recount.

With mum indoors, dad would say, "Hold the blinking thing still, weak handed wally. Time this monstrosity has finished climbing, you'll need to shin up the stem while I tie the sod to a flagpole. And leave it alone this year."

"Don't know what you mean, dad."

"Yes, you do, lanky liar. You pick out the seeds and chew 'em. Next time you feel the urge, ask your mother for a thick crust with a lot of marge on."

Scramble over our back wall and you were in another world. Imagine a piece of waste ground as big as a football pitch, fringed with cascades of greenery from overgrown blackberry bushes. Central stood a tall beech tree, and beyond that a sycamore, both at least a hundred years old. Swathes of Michaelmas daisies and rosebay willowherb, interspersed with dock leaves, sorrel and swaying tall grasses, grew in this urban Eden. Too big to be the back garden of even the grandest house, I have no idea why this undeveloped patch of countryside was right there in the middle of London. Gentle sounds were heard here, alongside the drone of the traffic. The trees gave home to wood pigeons, who returned to it each year, a fond family, judging by the *roop roop* cooing they made in the branches high up.

Part of this paradise had been commandeered as a builder's yard, which was fortunate for me, as access was denied to strangers because of a high metal fence topped with spikes right round the perimeter. I, though, could play secretly at the weekends and evenings when the builders had gone home. I climbed the trees, gathered and ate the blackberries, and imagined myself as an intrepid explorer in an undiscovered land.

Mother was as vigilant as ever about my forays 'over the wall'. "If you meet any strangers over there, you are to come back home immediately. There's some funny types about, these days!"

"No-one can get in. There's a big fence all round."

"That may be so, but there's ways and means how people can get in, and a boy on his own..."

"Oh, mum!"

A heavy sigh. "Well, just you do as I tell you, and no going near that old house!"

Far over the wasteland crumbled pitifully a once-splendid townhouse with a long strip of garden enclosed by a red brick wall. I think I must have been the only boy in Hammersmith who had scaled that wall and knew what the garden contained. At the far end of this secret garden was a blue-painted gazebo, almost hidden by a sprawling chestnut tree and surrounded by raspberry bushes that yielded soft and luscious fruit. The gazebo was door-less, and on entering I breathed in the damp smell of rotting floorboards mixed with the mustiness of old paper. Pinned to the slat walls of the old gazebo were picture postcards, distinctively separated into two categories: simple views; and provocatively-posed pictures of the nubile lovelies who graced the Edwardian stage. On the opposite walls were framed sepia photographs of fashionably plump velvet-clad principal boys, heroines-yet-heroes of some long-forgotten pantomime, the glass of the frames still intact.

Unpinned, the postcards bore laurel-wreathed halfpenny and carmine-red penny stamps. The postcard views had faded brown ink writing on the back from places like Frinton, Ventnor and Walton-on-the-Naze. 'We had a dip in the briny this morning. Devilish cold. Cissie sends her regards.' 'Boarding house comfy. Weather top hole. See you soon, old top.' The conventionally acceptable phrases were dated, as were the cards, showing in faded sepia unremarkable views of a beach, or a market cross, or a clubhouse behind a golf links. The other cards, the poses, had no writing sullying the back. Perhaps they were amassed by an aficionado of the beautifully buxom female figure, the swollen amplitude of which would now bring hoots of derision from the lads in the gallery at the Shepherds Bush Empire. I stole away from the gazebo, wondering whether these musical hall darlings were still alive, if they were withered old ladies now, perhaps with their costumes still in a trunk or wardrobe somewhere, brought out now and again to be gently stroked with shaky hands.

I never attempted to enter the house itself. Dire warnings from mum had filled me with trepidation about possible intruders, living or otherwise.

Chapter 12

My First Pair of Long Trousers

Strange glances passed between mum and dad a day or two prior to my fourteenth birthday.

What was I getting? As if I didn't know. On the great day itself, I was up early, and, sure as rent day coming around, the shiny brown paper parcel sat waiting on the kitchen table, complete with annoying delaying tactic of miles of enfolding thin twine. Hurting my fingers, I strained on and broke the twine. I could not wait to open this present. It wasn't a present; it was my passport to the grown-up world.

I beheld the cheap pair of long grey trousers as Solomon looked on Sheba. This roughly run-up pair of shapeless drainpipes, hairy to the touch, the quick work of some underpaid machinist labouring in a backstreet shed, meant more to me than my beloved bike standing in the passage. I loved my new 'trucks' more than I glowed to see mum's indulgent smile, as I held them in front of my long pale legs, which thankfully would soon be hidden inside them.

"Try them on," urged mum.

"Now?" I still couldn't grasp the dawn of this fateful day.

I stepped into their clinging warmth, did up the fly buttons, and fastened to their hooks the pair of shiny metal clips. They fitted me well. 'Rejoice, young man! Get thee behind me, schoolkid! Today I become a man!' "Mum! Chuck away my short trousers! I've longed for today."

Turning about and beholding mum's careworn face, I liked not what I saw – hesitation. I divined a reluctance to tell me something, something I didn't want to hear. "They're for looking after, you know," she said. "You will have to be very careful not to get them dirty too quickly. You see, Stan... When they're in the wash... Well... Then, you will have to go back into shorts."

She was all 'well' this and 'well' that, but there was nothing well about it. The news hit me with all the force of a smack in the face. I might have known it, should have thought of the small economies which had brought me my beloved new trousers. A spare pair where these came from? It wasn't on for a while at least. Then and there, I resolved never would I don those hateful shorts again. Somehow, I had to get money to buy another pair of proper trousers, or two pair, or three pair – there simply had to be some to change into.

And so, my quest for trouser money began...

Selling firewood was one money-making scheme. I'd steal outdoors with our chopping axe stuffed up my jumper, then I'd do my rounds. Home and Colonial Stores, stalls in the market, Lipton's, the Co-Op greengrocers – they must all have got sick of me begging and whining for wooden boxes, each one potential cash in my fist. "You again! No, we haven't got any! Piss orf! In here every sodding day..."

Then, with a length of tough sisal, I'd drag over pavements and busy streets scores of heaped boxes from the multiple shops. There existed a sort of inlet at the top of my street, the entry to a furniture depository rear, its massive doors invariably barred. There I dragged my prizes, and, grimly, with a will, I chopped them up. Those snappy little tomato crates I could break with my bare hands. But a persistent ragamuffin like me, desperate for coin, was willing even to contend with the resistant wire holding together Dominion's cheese crates, marked with the fern leaf of New Zealand or Canada's map contours indelibly black at one end. The resultant pile of chopped sticks I viewed as so much wealth, to be duly translated into the terms of new trousers, if I worked hard flogging them in bundles to the wealthier housewives of Barnes or Chiswick.

I got into the swing of lugging the biggest crate obtainable in the direction of these plutocrat suburbs, my bumping Ark afloat with its massed cargo, which I'd arranged as neatly as I could.

Ah, the housewives of Barnes and Chiswick... There were one or two pleasant old girls, admittedly, but for the most part they were niggardly, and ready, oh so ready, to do down a young 'un who must have seemed eager to sell.

"Penny a bundle? I get my wood from the shop at that price. Where's the bargain?"

"Missus, my bundles are bigger than what you'd get at the oil shop."

"I'll give you a penny for two bundles."

"What! That's not fair! And I've come all the way from Hammersmith."

I'd watch as the mean-eyed creature produced a fat purse from the pocket of a good suit jacket, her twin-setted bosom swelling at the thought of triumphing over the eager lad.

The firewood scheme was not my only idea to build up my spare long trousers fund. I took a Saturday job with a greengrocer over at Barnes, cycling furiously in all directions delivering the smallest of orders to parvenus who couldn't carry anything away with them with Poochie the Pomeranian in the loving clasp of their scented arms, taking a mere two pounds of plums three miles for their feeling inspection by a heavily powdered matron who wore, along with her expensive clothes, a disapproving expression…

"Young man, these look bruised to me. Not at all as when I bought them. Are you sure you didn't drop them on your way here?" She'd pause to deplore and sniff at my denial. "Take them back and return with sound ones. Really! I'll have to have a word with your employer."

For all these errands on my bike (out as far as Richmond on one occasion) and for sweeping the floor at the end of the day, I got the princely sum of half a crown for the whole Saturday's graft.

I added to my fund in whatever way I could. I helped market traders shutter up their stalls late at night, while my parents fretted on my absence. I regularly visited a score of telephone boxes, to press 'Button

B' in the hope of retrieving forgotten coins. And I found a trading outlet for comics in the playgrounds of Chiswick – our kids sold their read comics for a halfpenny each, but over Chiswick they were willing to buy copies without jammy thumb marks for a whole penny.

Finally, gloriously, my trousers reserve was all that it should be.

But that wasn't the end of my money-making drive. My trousers situation may have been resolved, but, as dad had always said, with long trousers came greater freedom, and now I found I had a better ambition in mind – paying for the pictures: the pictures with an actual girl!

Her name was Annie. The rough romance had begun one murky evening when the old man nodded off over the remains of chewed kipper bones and mum's vigilance slipped. I slipped also – along the passage and out the door, and discovered the street gang dividing up bodies into male and female for a more mature game of Hide and Seek which went by the provocative name of Kiss Chase. The name tells the tale. Shrewd, provocative eyes watch where the fancied filly trots off to, count one hundred off in fives, then follow, and track down a pair of wet lips in a basement. The bother with Kiss Chase was that any soft goon who returned to the rendezvous too soon found everyone else missing. For hours. There must be a few kids in the world today who owe their origins to Kiss Chase.

I fancied Annie strong. She was pushing fourteen, with firm little breasts like rounded apples under her jumper. And I wanted to handle the fruit. She had slightly prominent upper front teeth, had smiled shyly at me when I had joined the rest of the learner lovers, her come on that of a sexy rabbit inviting coy play.

She had gone to ground in the basement of one of the big houses, the occupant known to be away. I felt her top teeth impress a little as our mouths merged, and the little apples I examined thoroughly. I quickly discovered that Annie was a borderline case, the border being her waistline. Anything below that she was going to keep to herself. But she agreed to make a date for the pictures.

I longed to get into the exploratory back row, where the coats came off and were used like tents, all sorts going on beneath them, spread so that the undulating row of cloth heaved and bucked frequently. Any usherette flashing her torch would have thought animals were alive under the coats, and the buggers just wouldn't stay still.

Think of it! The pictures with Annie! I had only to amass two shillings for each trip – four pennies for our bus rides there and back, four more for each seat at the pictures, and afterwards a treat of a fish supper in the 'Cosy Corner', a tanner each.

So, I became acutely aware that with the donning of my long trousers began the first stirrings of my transition from innocent boyhood to sexual curiosity.

Chapter 13

The Best Laid Plans of Mice and Men

It was my own stupid fault that I went back to square one. I had gone to the pictures with Annie, spent the requisite amount of money on her, and enjoyed some erotic fumblings under my school mac in the back row. I now had my second pair of long trousers, and my hard-earned money was all used up, but I didn't need it any more. Life was looking good. But... 'The best laid plans of mice and men gan oft aglay' - so wrote the poet, and so it was with me...

I had no intention of ever wearing short trousers again. They could stay in the bottom drawer of the big wardrobe in mum and dad's room (my little room was too small for a wardrobe).

"If you want to go scavenging over that back wall into that bit of builder's yard, you put your shorts on, you hear?" said mum. She knew that dad was always wanting screws and nails, doorknobs and handles, anything that could be salvaged from the wasteland of window frames and doors wrenched from houses demolished, and that I always got the job of scavenging for them. Sunday mornings, when the builders had gone from the yard, I would be sent over our end wall to roam among the debris. Such a sadness appertained over there, the strewn decaying memorials to households which had known laughter and the happy sounds of children playing now declined, scabrous and unused. I always took pincers with me, as I wandered among the paths, treacherous with broken glass. There were long nails to be pulled, hooks to be unscrewed, all useful ironmongery for dad's carpentry.

Of course, I paid no heed to mum's warnings, and the next time I was sent over the wall, it was in long trousers...

The inevitable happened. A precarious pile of slates covered one door, the brass doorknob of which gleamed, inviting. Quite a prize! As I inched over the door, ready to retrieve said doorknob, I slipped and fell against a large nail sticking out, and felt the material of my trousers rip catastrophically from hip to knee. I paid no heed to any personal injury. I don't think I would have cared if I had broken a leg. All I could think of was the ruin of those trousers, such a huge rip that I doubted mum, even with her darning skills, could mend it.

I returned home with a bunch of nails and screws and a good pair of hinges. I forlornly hoped that these prizes might do something to alleviate the damage done to my good trousers.

I opened the back door. Mum was in the scullery.

"Mum, I've found some..."

"What have you done to your trousers!" she shrieked. "I told you that if you wanted to go over there you had to wear your shorts!"

"I hurt myself bad," I mumbled. Unfortunately, there was no blood, the material having saved me from physical harm.

Mum turned me right round, looking for blood or signs of injury. "Nothing wrong with you. No bruises, nothing. Go up to your room.

Dad will be back soon from Uncle Ned's, and he'll have something to say about this!"

With absolute dread I waited for dad coming back. Suppose he stopped my pocket money? The *sprarsi* (a sixpence) he gave me each week was generous for the time, and could buy a seat in the pictures plus sweets, or three comics. Since I had met Annie, I intended to save up so I could take her to the pictures about every three weeks or so, but if he stopped my pocket money…

Worse than that came the horrible realisation that with only one pair of long-'uns, I would sometimes have to go to school in short trousers, walk along our street in short trousers, let Annie see me in short trousers, my uncovered long white legs an obscenity in my eyes.

I heard dad's key in the lock. There were hasty mumblings between dad and mum. Then, "Stanley, get yourself down here at once!"

Dad glowered at me when I went down. "What's this I hear about you tearing your good trousers?"

"Dad, if you buy me a new pair, I won't want anything for my birthday, or Christmas or…" I tailed off, realising that what I had uttered so desperately had only made things worse.

"Buy you a new pair!" roared dad. "Buy you a new pair? I'm not buying you a new pair. You've made your bed and so you must lie on it. Those trousers are ruined, so you'll have to wear your shorts as spares until you earn enough money to buy yourself a new pair!"

And so resumed my quest for spare trouser money…

I recommenced the paper round, the chopping-up of boxes, the little errands here and there, and, because of my desperate need for money, I was forced to fall into the clutches of The Prophet.

The Prophet lived in one of the basement flats on the other side of our road. Now, I would hazard a guess that for most people the word 'prophet' conjures up an image of a man in swirling robes, with long white beard and hair to match, eyes agleam, standing on top of a mountain. Not so The Prophet who lived near us. He wore wire-rimmed glasses, had slicked down brilliantined hair, and bore a passing resemblance to Dr. Crippen, the famous poisoner. Everybody was afraid of him. He was in the habit of leaping out at boys passing by to declare, "Women are a snare and a delusion!" or, "The wages of sin is death!" The smaller boys he would clutch by the arm, and hiss in their face, "The mouth of the loose woman is a pit. Fall not into it!"

When younger, I had been accosted by him several times, but now I was taller he did not grab me on passing, but merely yelled, "The lips of the loose woman drip honey, but she is a two-edged sword!"

On this particular day, I was on my way, trundling the wooden crate of sticks I intended to sell, when out jumped The Prophet in front of me. "I'll take six bundles!" he bellowed.

"Six bundles?"

"Yes, boy, six. But you'll have to come down into the flat while I look for some money."

I hesitated. I was afraid, but tempted by the thought of money coming so easily. Reluctantly, I followed him down the steps. The room was very shabby: a worn moquette armchair, a scratched table, a dilapidated bookcase with a few magazines, very little else.

"Sit there, boy!" He pointed to the armchair, and dragged a battered kitchen chair across the dirty carpet and sat in front of me. From the top of the bookcase he took a cream tin. "You know what's in here?"

I did know, but did not want to admit it. Everyone knew what The Prophet dealt in.

"French letters!" he bellowed. Then he dropped his voice almost to a whisper. "These will save you from the fallen woman. Woe to the fallen woman! She is full of disease, and she will ruin you, destroy you and make you mad, insane!"

I quaked. Condoms. As everyone knew, he sold them to barber's shops, where the proprietor might ask, "Something for the weekend, sir?" before offering one to a customer. Better that than going to a chemist, where a young lady might serve you.

"Stay away from the fallen woman," The Prophet went on. "Shun her. But I know you won't. You young men – your brains are in your cock!"

I wondered how much longer I would have to endure the ravings of this repetitive fanatic before he got me my money and I could be on my way. "Sir, you wanted six bundles of sticks and..."

"All in good time. There are more important things. Babies!"

"Babies?"

"Yes, babies! How many unwanted poor little mites are brought into this world? These," he tapped the tin, "these could stop all those babies being born out of wedlock."

I had to admit that made sense. In those days, there were dire consequences for the unmarried girl who got pregnant. She was urged by her family to marry, and many young couples, not long ago children themselves, had to move in with resentful parents, the teenage father responsible not only for the demands of a baby, but also desperate to earn enough money to move his new family out, perhaps to get a room in a crumbling tenement in somewhere like seedy Notting Hill.

"Excuse me, sir, but..."

"All right, all right, I'll get you your money. But remember, if ever you want a rubber, a French letter, you know where to come. Me, I'm doing the world a service. Saving men from horrible venereal diseases where you're covered in sores and your nose drops off. Remember that, the next time you feel the urge!"

At last I got away, six bundles of sticks lighter, but with a heavy heart. The Prophet's words had reminded me of another man from the area, the one everybody shunned when he walked along the King Street. Where his nose should have been were just two gaping holes, the hideous legacy of untreated syphilis before the discovery of penicillin.

As I walked along, dragging my cargo behind me, I felt as if I wanted a good bath. But I cracked on. I headed for Barnes, across Hammersmith Bridge to the pleasant roads with their plane trees, and the gardens with their laurel bushes and shrubs.

"Tradesman's entrance, boy, tradesman's entrance," barked an imperious, matronly woman, who had opened her impressive, porticoed front door. "Cook may need some sticks for the fire. See her."

Cook did not want any sticks, and was as imperious as her employer.

It was then that I met a real lady. She was not much to look at, as she stood at her front door. She was dressed in an old, black, silk dressing gown, and her unpermed white hair stuck out in all directions.

"Well, young man, you look hot and bothered. Would you like a glass of lemonade?"

I would have given my right arm for a glass of lemonade. "Thanks, missus, I would."

"Come in and sit yourself down."

I was led into a room which spoke of a colonial past. On the wall were two crossed spears and a large wooden African mask. There was a bamboo table, and a smaller table with a brass top, on which was a heap of yellow pears. She motioned me to sit down on a faded velvet armchair. Through the French windows at the far end of the room, I could see the spreading branches of an old pear tree. As I sipped my lemonade nicely, she said, "We've had a lot of pears this year. Would you like to take some home?"

My first thought was that she meant in lieu of the money for the sticks. Not so.

"Oh, and the sticks. I'll take four bundles. Here's the money."

She actually gave me the pears for free. She put them in a brown paper bag and said, "Only too pleased they're going to a good home. Bye, dear."

I could hardly believe it, as I dragged my empty crate back over the bridge. Could posh people actually be nice?

When I got home, the pears went some way towards thawing the hearts of mum and dad over the ripped trouser episode.

I said, "This woman spoke ever so posh, but she was really nice. She had this old black dressing gown on, and..."

"Of course she was nice, son – because she was a real lady. Well-bred. People like her don't even have to try. They've just got class. Not like these parvenus."

"What's a parvenu, dad?"

"An upstart," interjected mother. "Nouveau riche. You know, like that woman who lives in Bridge Avenue, the one with the poodle."

I knew only too well.

Chapter 14

Forbidden Territory

Dad had not stopped my pocket money. I still got my sixpence on a Friday night, but there'd be no pictures or sweets until I managed to amass enough for new trousers.

Mum took pity on me. "I'll give you two-pence for every job you do while I'm away at my little job. The food safe needs tidying. Wipe the sauce bottles, clean the shelves. The brass tap needs polishing, and you can clean the fender. Tidy the drawer of the dresser, but don't throw anything away. You never know what might come in useful. And don't go in our bedroom. Nothing for you to do in there."

I waited for several moments after mum had shut the front door behind her. When I was sure she hadn't forgotten anything and would be away for at least a couple of hours, I went up to her bedroom.

Supposedly out of bounds to me unless I were invited in, mum and dad's bedroom received regular visits from me when I was temporary caretaker of 29 Angel. Then came a time of opening drawers, lifting lids, squeaking towards me the doors of the vast double wardrobe of figured oak. Inside, Dad's pearl-grey best trilby was shelved over his squarely shouldered brown suit, making, to my eyes, an upright ghost of a man, standing in readiness for an evening at the Buffaloes lodge.

On the other side of the wardrobe, mum's cherry military-cut coat showed me its black fur cuffs, a matching pair of black gloves protruding from its pocket.

Among the arrangement of far too much furniture for an easy navigation about the room rose a bamboo table, a carved teakwood chest and a whatnot thing in sandalwood. The beloved pieces were there to remind dad of his service in Mesopotamia and India and other places full of heat and scorpions. Even the thick jerry under the bed had a Mespotish motif. I imagine the old man saw swaying palm trees whenever he dinged the china.

Mum's dressing table had a permanent dusting of Rachelle face powder, so anything lifted had to go back on a polished circle or square among peachy sand. I found her stocks of womanly whiffs exciting: her big bottle of eau de cologne, *Johann Maria Farina 4711*; her small bottle of *Evening in Paris* perfume. The cologne didn't taste bad in small sips. The bottle lurked among a miniature tuning fork scatter of steely blue hairpins.

It was a sexy room, my parents' kipping place. Open a stiffly resistant drawer and I could hold against my chest a brassiere apparently made from tent canvas concealing artfully bent wire. And there were Directoire knickers in eau de Nil silky stuff – I knew their description, having seen them in Ambrose Wilson's catalogue. They never looked as wide and baggy as this in the adverts, though. Expand out the waist – damn good elastic. I had best put them back exactly where they were.

The great iron bed dominates the scene. It's an imposing structure, with front and back rails hammered out in some ferrous foundry, looking like sections of organ pipes welded in hurdle design. Obscenely huge brass knobs top the bedhead like a robot lady's metal breasts with nipples pointing to the ceiling. The strung wire mattress frame can be made tauter if a thing like a car starting handle is forcibly and slowly wound. Turn the other way, and those reclining would end with bums touching the floor. The bed's in layers: wire mattress, goose feathers crammed into rough-striped ticking; then at least four blankets above the sheets, plus eiderdown; coverlet; and, last of all, dad's shapeless but warm army greatcoat. Easily see which side of the bed is dad's – his pillow is greasy from the smears of Vaseline with which he smears down his abundant and greying hair.

The bedside table supports a Germanic two-bell alarm clock. It dances pompously in chrome rotundity when the reverberating strikers set up their din. That *bomp* on the floor around ten to six every weekday morning is dad, jerked wrathful from dreaming of bathing naked in the Tigris with other Tommies needing an inferno day slosh, sending the clock flying with a punch. Another day's demanding work ahead.

In an alcove, deep one side of the bed, slumps dad's army kitbag. Drawing loose the skeined cords, I feel for the histories of his time as a surgeon's assistant in a field hospital tented on sand dunes. A tin inside was originally intended to preserve papers of gold leaf, but now keeps from foxing all the photographs dad took over there with his simple box camera: a bridge of boats on the Hooghly, dad wearing a topi, building a Dutch oven, and smiling to mates – that proves he wasn't always mopping up blood and passing scalpels.

The dirty brown ribbons of dad's winding puttees are in this dark recess bag. Perhaps he keeps them in masochistic memory? After all, they are responsible for the varicose veins that put an end to his dancing. "Round and round the lower leg, Private. That's right, we'll have you smart yet." It smarts with dad that round and round the slippy marble floor wasn't for him on demobilisation. A pair of heavy black boots; a chink of medals; a St. John's Ambulance Service handbook, with silver star emblazoned; a peaked cap in rough felting, with the dull badge of the Middlesex regiment... I stuff the whole issue back into darkness. Do I hear the faint sounds of a mournful bugle? Fight on, stout soldier. Fight poverty and need, the oppression of the masses... Is the class war any less of a struggle?

In the alcove leans a long bamboo cane attached to a flag. The proudly patriotic Union Jack, as big as a cot sheet, droops hangdog, enfolding itself, shabbily in need of a wash. Last year, I flourished this banner at the Silver Jubilee celebrations, when red, white and blue stripes erupted over the street architecture, stonework, brick and gatepost. I remember that the occupants in the house opposite even planted red salvias, white alyssum and blue lobelia. One other character bedaubed his Ford Ten to look like a giant garish humbug with blank glassy eyes. How strange is this spontaneous emotion which rises in the plebeian breast at instructed times for celebration? Our street sees the Royals as they do Clark Gable and Jean Harlow, as figures fabulous in the firmament, all stardust, wealth and fame, moving in expensive cars in a dazzlingly bejewelled existence.

Two steps from the fireplace takes me to the 'hobbies' cupboard. Atop the cupboard is a set of encyclopaedias. Find out about everything from what is an axolotl, to where Zanzibar is. Next to them, a fat, brown tome, *The Household Doctor*. A tickle in the throat, a wart on the wotsit, and whoever is afflicted flicks hurriedly and finds at least five dire diseases as the cause. I open the cupboard, and there's a smell of engine oil. My beautifully crafted train set. Or is it dad's? "Getting up steam now, boy. Look at the funnel. Listen! Water's well on the boil." The old man's eyes mirror the glow beneath the boiler. He's in a wonderland of boyhood recaptured.

On the top shelf of the cupboard stretches a mass of pulp – pulp magazines with terrific titles: *Amazing Stories*; *Weird Tales*; *Black Mask*; *Astounding*. Then there are piles of mags that are all galaxies and space travel, interplanetary wars and flying saucers, ray guns and deadly missiles. The men and women in these tales have lightning flashes on high leather boots, wear variations on Roman helmets (only without nose plate protection, visors or ear guards), and carry all sorts of unlikely devices.

But I have jobs to do. If I want to earn twopences, I have to tear myself away from the magazines and get cracking with some cleaning.

At last I stand on the threshold of the scullery and deplore what I see. The facilities in this den of discomfort are but a couple of moves from the domain of a Neanderthal cave-wife. The stone floor diffuses a permanent chill for feet, seeping through the coco-matting covering. The thick plaster walls peel and flake, leaving powdery deposits in the corners. The black-enamelled gas stove takes up so much room, with its thick, safe-like door, that an amply built person would have to breathe in to reach the whitewashed stone copper in the corner. This rises to the right of the heavy stone sink, looking like a blank-faced cliff, its great lid like a wheel from a wooden chariot. The copper has a grate below for the insertion of newspaper, sticks, coal. On Monday, washday, the fire roars, fierce as thunder, the iron door, swung out, reveals the incandescent blaze rushing to get up the chimney, while the clothes in the copper go *hubble-bubble, glop, hibble-hobble*, like the deep croakings of some nightmarish enormous toad.

One of my jobs is to rub up the brass tap over the sink. The gleam of it, burnished up with Brasso, reveals a crazy fairground distorting mirror for my face. I pull several grimaces before realising I haven't done very much of it and have a way to go before I finish.

The left-hand dresser drawer is always pleasingly tidy; it contains a folded ironing table cover bearing a scorch mark, Irish linen runners, and beautifully embroidered tablecloths, some wedding presents never used. There's nothing fascinating here, but there is the clean purity-personified smell – it's the smell mum exudes herself, so fastidious in her person, a would-be lady resigned to being a drudge of a housewife, a near-slave to the demands of a husband and son.

123

Dare I brave the right-hand dresser drawer, though? That always needs tidying. Everything surplus goes in there. Tidying it will earn me two-pence, so I tug open the drawer, and there's enough stuff in it to fill a jumped-on suitcase: odd gloves, woollen-limp and kid-soft; cards of navy blue and grey darning wool; this year's and last's *Old Moore's Almanack*; a pretty birthday card with glitter dust and a spray of pansies; more cards, with logs and robins and holly, possibly from a Yuletide when I was a baby; mothballs; marbles; an album for wild flower cigarette cards; reels of Coats cotton; rent books; insurance books; a fake silver charm of a little elephant from a Christmas cracker; paper chains still in their wrapper... I must get them all out of this drawer and hastily tidy the contents as best I can before mum comes home from her 'little job'.

By the time I heard her key in the lock, I had earned the magnificent sum of fourpence.

"What you've been doing all this time and only managed to get two jobs done I don't know," she said.

"It's that drawer, mum. There's so much in it, and I had to look through and sort things out, and..."

"Yes, I know, I know. Well, here's the fourpence I promised. Maybe you can find something more to do next week."

With chopping wood, running errands, doing my paper round, and taking on jobs for mum, I eventually achieved the goal I desired: at last I was able to buy myself a new pair of spare long trousers.

Chapter 15

Jobs, Grottoes and Books

I lost Annie to a delivery boy who worked for Palmer's grocery store.

He had a nice black bicycle which had green writing on it and a deep wicker basket. He was also earning money, and was able to treat Annie properly, whereas I had been saving hard to try to look like a little man in long trousers.

I strutted down the street, wanting to show off these hard-earned acquisitions, but the little boys playing in the street had no interest in the lanky schoolboy from number 29. My tormentors, those who had taken my sweets and comics but given me no friendship, had moved on into work.

Jobs seemed easy to come by in those days, most of the girls becoming shop assistants or working in cafés peeling potatoes and shucking peas for the cook, the boys becoming apprenticed to tradesmen, making the tea and sweeping up, learning the trade first-hand to become skilled men at eighteen.

There was no question of university or college. The spinster next door, who had a good job as a secretary, had probably stayed on for an extra year at school to learn shorthand and typing, or maybe been on a secretarial course. Middle class girls were not expected to work. They just hung about until they got married, spending their time changing their library books, or maybe doing crochet or embroidery at home, footling their life away. One of the girls who lived in one of the big houses near the King Street had reached her mid-thirties without marrying, and now prospects for her were slim. Her parents allowed her to give mandolin lessons for two and six a plucking hour.

Shortly before their children reached their fourteenth birthday, parents began to ask around about possible jobs. Older girls who worked in Woolworth's were approached: "Any jobs for our Lily or Mabel?" Men in the builder's yard were asked, "Any jobs going for our Fred? Good strong strapping lad, he is. He'd work hard!"

Unemployment was practically unheard of. "I'm not keeping you anymore, son. You get out and get yourself a job." This was the attitude of parents then.

I was feeling disappointed in the lack of interest in my trousers, when little Joycie Waites called out, "Oi, Stan! Got a new pair of long-'uns I see!"

Joycie, a thin little girl in a faded cotton frock and with a cardigan darned at the elbow, was a maker of grottoes. A grotto was an arrangement of assorted treasures, all of which could be found in the average home, very much like all the bits and pieces in our dresser drawer.

I crossed over the road to inspect her latest creation. "Fair old effort you've made there, Joycie."

She beamed proudly at the praise. The tawdry pavement shrine had a paper Union Jack at one corner, and, in front of the flag, seashells. It had coloured chalks, postcards of fat ladies having their arses nipped by a gleeful crab, baubly bits of broken costume jewellery, a daisy petal earring, pebbles spelling out Joycie's name, marbles, broken shards of patterned china, cotton reels with two or three wispy threads still clinging, and finally, in the middle of it all, the pièce de résistance, a plastic tortoiseshell slide displayed on a torn lace handkerchief.

"Penny for the grotto, Stan?" Joycie said, looking up hopefully. Several of the girls made grottoes like this, calling out to passers-by to donate for the privilege of seeing their work of art so carefully arranged.

I reached into my trouser pocket. Yes, luckily, I did have a penny there. I liked Joycie. She was so harmless and innocent, and soon it would be her fourteenth birthday and she would have to leave school and start work. No more grottoes for her then.

Joycie was lucky. She had a big sister, Lily, who worked in Orton's. This was a privileged position indeed. Orton's was a large haberdashery store with side windows that went back to make a kind of glass room, where all kinds of drapery items were displayed. The entrance hall had black and white tiles laid diagonally leading up to a glass fronted door. Inside were long oak drawers with glass knobs, containing ladies' drawers in pink, white, pale green and blue. Plaster dummies of bobbed-haired girls with disturbingly grinning teeth modelled liberty bodices or cotton vests. Brassieres were discreetly out of sight, stored away until somebody asked for them. There were lace hankies, gloves, scarves of all colours, stockings ranging from old ladies 60 denier Lisle to delicately sheer silk 15 denier creations. The shop assistants wore black dresses with white collars and their hair was always neat and tidy. They would write out the name of the items bought on a chit backed with a piece of carbon paper, and this, along with the cash from the customer, was put in a cardboard tube, screwed into a holder on a long piece of wire, and a handle pulled to send the tube winging its way to a cashier, who sat up in a little booth reached by a winding iron staircase. Orton's was an emporium, not a shop.

Joycie's birthday came and went. She finished school on the Friday and was working the following Monday, the job secured by her big sister. What a transformation was there! I saw her coming home from work, a little bit of discreet make up on, just a little lipstick and a touch of powder. Funny to think she was earning now, and me still at school.

I didn't really care about losing Annie. Evenings and weekends were taken up with study. I was now allowed the privilege of being able to use the hallowed front room.

"He needs quiet to concentrate, Sid. Can't concentrate with you listening to the wireless, or shuffling about turning over newspaper pages. Lots of work to do now he's got his scholarship."

In the sanctuary of the front room, how I read! I found Dickens entertaining. I could empathise with his exaggerated characters:

impossibly innocent Oliver Twist; Pip in *Great Expectations*; the villains like Magwitch, Bill Sykes and Fagin. But Scott, Sir Walter, I couldn't stand. Never wrote two words where ninety-seven would do! Lines and lines of description about a knight: helmet, armour, sword, dagger, caparisoned horse, and God knows what else, the elaborate description holding up the action.

Scott we had to read for school, but left to my own devices I read for pleasure. One of my favourite books was *The Last Falaise*, a schoolboy saga about a youthful individualist in a snobby college for chinless wonders who had a blazing temper over some imposition unjust. And I also liked Sir Arthur Conan Doyle's Sherlock Holmes stories.

Anything in print I never threw away. In my bedroom, deep cardboard cartons held my own history of prowess in reading from being very small. First, the weighty wonderment of a *Chums* annual. This had been a super Christmas present; hundreds of fine-drawn illustrations, adventure, enchantment, and tingling excitement, all in page after smoothly-turned page. Then *Tansy and Bobbles on Fable Island*, *Weary Willie and Tired Tim*, and Laurel and Hardy in *Film Fun*, Stan with his hapless smile, Ollie's eyebrows joined together in exasperation. I had even saved *Sunny Stories*, a twee treat for little children all about elves and fairies.

Mum once opened the door, offering a cup of tea and cake. "Stan!" she admonished. "What on earth are you doing reading *Sunny Stories*? You're fourteen, not four! Shouldn't you be reading something a bit more intellectual?"

"Just reminiscing, mum."

"All right, son," she said softly, and she left the tea and cake and closed the door quietly behind her.

Chapter 16

A Nasty Piece of Work

Stan Drewitt was a nasty piece of work.

A lad of sixteen, he had a good job as a measurer of inside legs in the fifty bob tailors, and he always wore a smart pinstriped suit. He had probably got the job because of his looks. I had to admit it, he was good looking. His fair hair was sleeked down with lavender brilliantine, he had harebell blue eyes, and full lips that were rather too red for a boy (kissable lips, as Lily Waites had said). Face of an angel, heart of a devil. Drewitt was a twister of arms behind backs, a kicker of ankles.

He lived with his inoffensive widowed mother, a careworn but pleasant woman. She took in washing and went out scrubbing floors to earn a crust. I don't think her son gave her much money. Not that he couldn't afford it. I saw him counting ten bob notes, and even one- or two-pound notes, sometimes.

One day, as I was admiring one of Joycie's grotto creations, he stopped close by and studied the arrangement of buttons and feathers surrounding a jar of wilting laburnums plucked from a bush in Bridge Avenue.

"Lovely, Joycie," he said. "Very good effort. Reckon it deserves a penny, don't you, Stan?" His smile was a twisted sneer.

I nodded eagerly, and croaked, "Yes." Mustn't offend him.

He laid a coin down on the pavement and sauntered away.

Joycie picked up the coin, and her expression quickly changed from one of pleasure to one of angry disappointment, and she came out with the worst expletive she could think of. "Oi, you, Drewitt, rotten ox! This 'ere's an Irish penny!"

"Well, to be sure, it is, mavourneen," he replied, in a mock Irish accent. "I gave you a penny, didn't I? Didn't say it was going to be an English penny, did I? Use it to buy a sprig of shamrock to pretty up your shitty grotto!"

I winced for Joycie. If I'd had a penny in my pocket at the time, I would have given it to her.

It happened one Saturday afternoon that mum had run out of a particular shade of lavender for her embroidery.

"Stan," she called. "Want to do an errand? I've looked in Woolworth's and they haven't got the shade I want. Go over to the haberdasher's in Barnes and see if they've got any. I'll give you a bit of thread to match. Make sure it's an exact match, mind!"

I didn't mind the errand. I liked the walk over Hammersmith bridge to Barnes, liked the big red brick Harrods Furniture Depository, looking so grand and imposing, liked the gracious houses along the mall, a magnolia tree in one garden, a purple wisteria winding its way round a balcony in another. If I leaned over the bridge and watched the barges floating down below, it gave me a swimmy feeling, as if I wanted to jump down onto one of them and sail away down the Thames.

Hammersmith. Some said the name came from 'Hamer's hythe', after a Dane who landed there centuries ago. Others told the story that long ago a duchess was riding through the countryside in her carriage when the wheel came off, and, as it was being mended by the local blacksmith, she was said to call impatiently, "Hammer, smith!" All conjecture, of course, but these were the thoughts I had as I hurried across the bridge to Barnes.

I completed my mission; the embroidery thread was successfully obtained. So, I headed back home for afternoon tea. What could possibly go wrong?

Standing at the foot of the bridge was Stan Drewitt. It was his afternoon off, and he was dressed in all his ostentatious glory. I both feared him and admired his sense of style.

Freed from his need to look tastefully dressed for work, he seemed to be following the current trend towards Chicago gangster fashion. His camel hair overcoat had its collar turned up, even on this fairly mild day. He wore one white kid glove and held the other in the gloved hand swankily. He was smoking a fat, oval, mildly whiffy Teofani Turkish fag. Outside of his coat hung the double tongues of a white scarf, fringed silk. His trousers, twenty-three inches wide at the bottoms, were a bright Saxe blue, his shoes co-respondent brown and white with punched hole design.

I began to quicken my pace, wanting to get past him as quickly as I could, but as I was about to run past him with a timid glassy smile, he deliberately stepped into my path so that I cannoned into him.

"Hold it! Look where you're going!" He put his big shoe on my small foot, imprisoning me where I stood.

"I'm sorry, Stan!" I whimpered.

"Mister Drewitt to you," he said.

"I'm sorry, Mister Drewitt. Mum's at home waiting for me, and, well... I'm sorry."

"So you ought to be." Soft fingers with well-manicured nails reached out and plucked from the crescent neck of my pullover the propelling pencil which had been clipped there, the body of the pencil concealed. The slender article was russet brown, and, when Drewitt rotated it, in tinfoil hue lettering was revealed 'Silver Jubilee 1910-1935'.

"Where d'you get this, kid? Half-inch it?"

"No, I got it at school. We all got one, and a mug, too, with the king and queen's pictures on."

Stan Drewitt manipulated the top of the pencil, where the rotary fitment sent forth a peep then retreat of sharpened lead. "Nice. Elegant, like. Bet you think a lot of it."

"Yes."

"A pity that. I don't know what's come over me today, kid. I got this urge to send things skimming out over the water. Not long ago, I got rid of a bloody good hat because a seagull shit on the brim. You see, that offended me. Like you offended me a bit ago, old mate, not watching where you were going and barging into me. So, here goes!"

Like a russet dragonfly, in hurled rejection the pencil flew in a smooth arc to dip the other side of the embankment wall. Its fast trajectory carried it across the muddy foreshore, the tide having ebbed out across the mud grey flats. The keenest ear would have picked up no sound at all as the treasured pencil sank to obscurity.

Letting me have my foot back, Stan gently pushed up my chin with gloved hand.

"Huh!" he derided contemptuously on seeing the bravely unspilled tears reluctantly flooding my eyes. "Things like souvenirs going up the spout happen when you bump into me, son. Another time, you'll watch out, and walk, not run, past me, respectful. Now hop it!"

He knew I wouldn't tell. You didn't snitch. It was an unwritten rule. I didn't want any trouble, just a quiet life. Should have turned back and gone back to Barnes when I saw him. Had a walk round till he'd gone.

I walked back past the boathouse, where knobbly-kneed public school boys were hovering about a slim racing hull. They spoke loudly, informative to no-one really attentively listening, as if stencilling their blah-blah words on the stirring breeze.

"I thought it a particularly spiffing day for a scull, Roger."

"I'll say. Top hole!"

Gate-mouths. Haw-haw superior, their lazy drawl. Their thick woolly sweaters were an upper-class uniform, their speech as varnished as their boats. Even their names were superior. No Alfs, Berts, or Freds. They were Quentin, Rupert, or James (never shortened to Jimmy).

Sauntering on, calming myself down from the shock encounter, I soon reached Clark's Lead Mills. A barge was in, sunk low. Puffing and panting labourers continually cut across the alleyway, jog-trotting over springy planks, bent way down by the weakening weight of the formidably heavy, dull ingots they bore on their padded shoulders. The men for the most part had leaden, depressing expressions themselves, their prospects in life as grey as the metal itself. They wore baggy, saggy, dust-dark clothes. An anonymous trot of weary wage slaves egging on tired muscles from one thin pay packet to the probable (but not definite) next. How could they do what they did for such poor reward? Years of it loomed ahead – if they were lucky. Better this than the humiliation of being out of work.

Should be hurrying back now, or mum would be getting anxious, and I could do without another altercation. But I stopped to suck in water from the fountain opposite the top of Bridge Avenue. I wanted to wash away any remnants of tears, but the splash of intensely cold droplets unnerved me. Trickles of cold water about my face worried me no end. At home, I never sluiced my features. I always used a flannel. Sluicing and splashing under a running tap got me into a stupid, gasping fright. It was as if, in the cold spurting onslaught of the icy water running and dribbling down my features, I could actually feel my face dissolving, my nose, my lips, my eyes all gone.

I shivered off these thoughts as I crossed the road to Ship Lane. I cut through the cobbled entry near where I had, as a kid, scrabbled for ice chips. They fell from the great blocks of ice that Togni's Ice Works employees manfully manoeuvred on chained pincer contraptions.

When I turned abruptly into Angel Road, I peeped in on the old cobbler, working away, waxed thread between his lips, hammer descending and rising rapidly. In his window stood a statuette clothed in dust-specked white trousers, straw hat and bow tie, perpetually grinning a melon-slice smile at the back of a hillock of boots and shoes. Rumour had it that this figure was hollow, and was stuffed with the miserly old craftsman's hard-earned savings. I put my face to the window, watching the dedicated slave at work, when his shrewd, rheumy old eyes looked up at me, seeming to say, "Sod off, boy, I'm busy."

"You've been a long time. Where have you been?" said mum as she answered the door.

"Just for a walk, mum. Got the thread."

It was an exact match, and appeased mum. Later, in the quietness of my room, I tried to concentrate on the latest adventures of Dan Dare in my comic, but I found myself brooding about Stan Drewitt. Only two years my senior, and yet he had the power to humiliate me. I had felt intimidated by the smartness of his clothes, envied his rakish air and confidence. His clothes had made him feel like that, and I had felt so young in my grey flannel trousers and grey pullover. I had yearned for my long trousers, had worked so hard to get them. But, after all the trouble I had taken, they had suddenly lost their appeal.

What I wanted more than anything now was a suit.

Chapter 17

The Importance of Getting a Suit

It was always good to come back to 29 Angel, my home, my sanctuary.

I was subdued from my encounter with Drewitt, and rested my head on my arms, sitting at the large pine table in the kitchen. We called this room the kitchen, though most people would probably have called it the living room. In our house, though, it was often used for kitchen-related jobs, because the marble-topped table in the scullery was so small. Mum would often come through to use the big pine table for such jobs as shucking peas, sifting flour into bowls, or feeding chunks of leftover Sunday roast through the clamped-on mincer to make mince for a succulent shepherd's pie. Hence, our living room we called the kitchen.

On this particular day, mum was in the scullery, gushing water into a kettle, and when she stepped through into the kitchen, I was so caught up in my ruminating at the table that I didn't hear her.

"Funny boy," she said, ruffling my hair. "Sitting there and thinking. Miles away, you were. What are you thinking about?"

"What's for tea, that's all." Now I was lying. It was hard to tear myself away from thoughts of a suit.

I had to stop thinking. Dad would be in soon. He always did the same thing when he came in: fling the *Evening News* on the table, and look about for the cat to say hello to first. Dad could have done with a reprimand for this; such a mistake to stroke Betty's head before finding a smile and word for mum.

There was always a cat at 29 Angel. I am fairly certain that my father bestowed on each successive creature the affection intended for the little sister I never had. My parents maintained a secrecy on the subject of why I was the only child. I asked once, and was evasively answered. I assumed shamefully that mum didn't want the risk of a carbon copy of me doubling the harassment.

Cats! Cats on the table; cats underfoot; an untrained kitten from a wild litter of warehouse mousers, which ran up the curtains one side and down the other... Peter, ancient and eventually incontinent, was taken to be put to sleep by mum when dad was at work, and was so beloved by dad that, when he discovered the awful truth, he wouldn't speak to mum for a week, and, as we were between lodgers at the time, went to sleep in the spare room.

When we'd had tea, dad would sit in his Windsor armchair by the window and listen to the wireless. This particular day was no exception. I, still sitting at the table and having done all my homework, appeared to be listening to it, too, until dad roared at some joke, said, "That's a good 'un, I say, that's a good 'un, Stan!" and I failed to respond.

"What's the matter with you, Dreamy Daniel?" he said, impatiently. "Off in the land of Timbuktu, miles away. What you thinking about?"

Before I could stop myself, I blurted out, "Suit."

"What d'you mean, 'suit'? What kind of suit? Gentleman's suit? Suit of cards? You're too young to be thinking about suits."

"But there's some nice suits in the fifty bob tailor's, dad." Some of the boys who were earning now had actually saved up enough money after a few months' hard graft to afford such a £2 10s suit (£2.50 in today's money) from the establishment on the corner at the junction of Bridge Avenue and King Street.

"You've got your school uniform, and you won't be needing a suit for a good while yet. When you get your first job, you'll be wearing a jacket and your school flannel trousers. Then you can save up to get yourself a suit."

And that was that. Mum then started recounting for the old man the fascinating events of her day, such as how she had managed to find the cufflink he'd lost after crawling nose down all round the bedroom mats. All the while, Woody, our grey and white tabby, was on dad's knee, and as mum was talking, dad was stroking the cat, playing with its ears, chucking its chin, rubbing its head, and now and then mewing daftly to it, like he was the cat's real father.

At last, mum lost her temper. "Will you stop that! You'll have that cat as daft as yourself with all your silly fussing. Think you must have been a cat yourself in a previous life!"

All this was happening as if in a dream far away. All I could see in my mind's eye was me swanking down the road in a pinstriped suit.

Mentally, I dressed myself like little girls put cut-out cardboard dresses on paper dolls. First, the pinstriped suit, a nice ginger colour with brown stripes. Next, the wide-striped shirt, brown and yellow. A brown tie with embroidered leaves in red and gold. A nice pair of brogues, brown and white, with punched hole decoration. Red silk socks with zig zags. Then, add the rest of the outfit. A heavy camel hair coat with leather buttons. A white silk-fringed scarf. A brown felt fedora with a red ribbon hat band, worn at a rakish angle, slanted over one eye. That would show Stan Drewitt.

Then the wonderful realisation occurred to me: if I did save up enough money to buy myself a suit, Stan Drewitt would have to serve me. When I entered the shop, he would have to approach me and say, "Good morning, sir. Can I help you?" Under the watchful eye of his boss, he would have to measure my inside leg, and grovel at my feet while he did it. Oh, what bliss that would be! Stan Drewitt: my subordinate. I needed fifty bob now like fish need water.

Already I had flogged myself to death with two arduous rounds of money earning. The prospect of doing all the same old tasks again wearied my soul. How could I get enough to be the means of humiliating Stan Drewitt? I sighed so heavily that mum and dad stopped whatever they were talking to each other about and looked over at me.

"No good sighing like that son. Told you you're too young. Still a schoolboy. Concentrate on your studies. Get yourself a well-paid job when you leave."

"I do concentrate on my studies, dad."

"He does, Sid," mum chimed in.

I didn't want to wait a year to get my own back. If there was a way to get money easily, I wanted to know about it.

Fate has a strange way of lending a hand…

I had almost given up the idea of ever getting the better of the odious Stan Drewitt, when, coming back from school a few weeks later, I saw a spotted green and white silk scarf fluttering in the gutter. I picked it up and felt it. It was real silk, not rayon, and felt soft and delicate. Mentally, I could add it to my dream wardrobe. Tucked into a silk eau de Nil shirt, it would look sporty teamed with a pair of cream pleated-top trousers.

There was only one person who it could belong to, and that was Vince. Imagine a man of about forty-two, someone a cross between Flash Harry of *St. Trinian's* fame and Errol Flynn. Oily good looks, a pencil-thin moustache, broad shoulders, a slim waist enhanced by a close fitting belted camel hair coat. Vince always wore a pork pie hat, either green, brown or maroon. Always wore a scarf, too, always silk. It might be spotted, striped, zig zagged or plain, but it was always silk. There was no-one else down the street this particular scarf could belong to. Returning it might get me a *joey* (a threepenny bit) or even a *sprarsi*. I supposed it was a start.

Boldly, I knocked at his front door. It was opened wearily by his long-suffering wife, Louise. She always seemed to be wearing a grey suit. Whether it was always the same one or not, I don't know. She wore it with a twinset and pearls, and she never wore a pinny. She was smoking, as usual, and her heavy, bloated features and weary eyes spoke of once reasonable looks ruined by alcohol. It was whispered among the other housewives that Vince had a woman living up the West End – Mayfair, they thought. She was reputed to be quite a bit older than him and owned an exclusive boutique. Perhaps his fancy clothes, silk shirts and expensive suits, and his little green Hillman, the only car in the street, came from her generosity. Vince was a market trader, had a stall up Shepherds Bush Market, dealing in little knickknacks of every kind, but his reputed side-line as a gigolo seemed more lucrative.

"Yes?" said Louise languidly, between puffs on her Woodbine.

"I've found this scarf in the street. Thought it might belong to Mr. Collins."

"Probably does. I'll give him a shout. Vince! Boy here to see you. Stan Tinsley!"

"What does he want?" came the response, uttered from the depths of the house.

"Scarf. Thinks it's yours."

"Might be."

Vince came to the door with a glass of beer in his hand. He had an ordinary cotton shirt on, old grey trousers, and braces dangling. He didn't bother to get dressed up for Louise. He only looked smart when he was going out. "Yes, it is mine. I like that scarf. Glad you found it, son."

He looked quite kindly at me, and I was hopeful for a reward. What that reward would be I could never have guessed in my wildest dreams.

"You seem quite a reliable sort of a lad. How'd you like to help me with my stall on a Saturday? Nice Saturday job for you, if you want it? Means getting up early, mind. I want to be away by seven. Load stuff into the car, serve on the counter. Good at sums, are you?"

"Oh yes, sir!" I lied enthusiastically. "Very good!"

"Right, well, be round at the front door on Saturday, quarter to seven sharpish, and we'll be at the stall till evening, six-ish, thereabouts. I'll give you ten shillings for the day."

Ten shillings! It was a king's ransom. Five weeks and I'd have my suit. Ten shillings! It was as if St. Peter had come down from the sky and offered me the keys to Heaven.

All I needed now was dad's permission, and I was prepared to grovel, beg, do every odd job I could think of to get it. Ten shillings! I couldn't wait.

Chapter 18

My Job with a Dodgy Geezer

"You're not going to help Vince Collins on his trashy stall, and that's final!" roared dad.

"But, dad..."

"You're not going to hang about with him like some corner boy!" 'Corner boy' was a grave insult, meaning the worst kind of lowlife, up to no good, ne'er-do-well.

"But, dad, he's all right, and he'll bring me there and back in his car, and..."

"He won't, because you're not going."

"Sid, but Sid..." Mum was trying to get a word in edgeways, but all to no avail.

"You're a scholarship boy, not some spiv. I know what Vince Collins is like, slinking off up the West End servicing some rich bint!"

"Sid! Don't talk like that in front of the boy. And, well, it will give him a chance to improve his arithmetic. Actually working and having to handle money..."

"I'm surprised at you, Nance, supporting him. What about his homework?"

"He could do that on a Sunday."

"What about our walks in the country?"

"You could go by yourself."

"Why should I?"

Mum was firm. "Because the boy wants to use his initiative. He's only serving on a market stall, not robbing a bank."

I was amazed at mum's firm support.

"How much is Vince going to give you?" demanded dad.

"Ten shillings."

"Ten shillings!" Dad was impressed. "Well, maybe you could give it a try. But if you come up against any dodgy geezers, I want you to give it up, understand? I don't want you getting into bad company."

So it was that I was allowed to get up at six on a Saturday, dress as smartly as I could, and go around to wait for Vince. He came out with three big cardboard boxes that I struggled to load into the back seat of his car.

"Well, jump in, son. Don't hang about."

Ten minutes later, we were underneath the railway arch, cat-walking on duckboards behind the Shepherd's Bush market stall. It was early, and Vince was saving his spiel for later. One or two housewives drifted by, one stopping to hold up a cotton reel into the morning light, another removing a screw top from a bottle of cheap perfume to see if it smelled nice. Vince was dressed up. For his job, he wore a navy pinstripe suit, a blue shirt, and a navy-blue tie patterned with a scarlet pimpernel.

"Now," he said to me, "watch, look and learn. You've got to draw in the crowds. Convince them that there's something worth having." Then he turned to face the customers. "Now, come along there, ladies and gents," he began loudly. "Come this way for your household bargains. Spend over a shilling, you choose any tuppenny article free." He danced along the duckboards, drawing attention to the rows of scent bottles in fancy moulded glass shaped like animals. Here was a penguin wearing a scarf, a teddy bear with a tilted top hat on, a long-necked duck, beak agape, a cat sporting a pale blue-ribbon bow tie. He unscrewed a bottle and held it out to a passing woman. "Sniff that, lady. Lovely and flowery. Put some of that on the places where you're warmest in bed, and he'll think he's somewhere in Arabia lying next to Scheherazade!"

"Who she when she's out?" giggled the young mother, a sleeping child in her pushchair.

"An Eastern princess what told tales. You buy that scent and in a few months you'll come back here to tell me a tale: that you had to get rid of that pushchair for a double pram!"

She was not displeased. She produced a purse from her shopping bag. "Don't know 'bout that," she said, even as she handed over her money. "Me and Arthur don't want no more."

Vince gave her change from her florin. "Tell him to tie a knot in it, then. Or there's always what's under the counter, you know." He gave her a wink. "Oi, Stan, serve the lady at the end of counter!"

A heavy, middle-aged woman wearing a worn ribbed twill coat and with no stockings, showing the inky varicose veins in her mottled pink legs, asked apologetically, "Are these stockings guaranteed not to ladder easily?"

"I..." Hesitation from me.

But Vince interrupted. "Bless you, lady, the silkworms what spun them put cast iron glue in their jaws. Want to come back here and try 'em on? You'd get a testing legful and I'd get an eyeful."

"Young man, you are way too cheeky!"

I stood bewildered and amused by all the witty banter.

Vince looked at me and his expression changed. "Well, don't just stand there, young 'un! The lady wants her stockings wrapped up."

I reached for a brown paper bag and took her money. My work on the stall had begun.

We quickly found our roles: Vince was the comedian; I was the taker of money and wrapper of parcels.

It soon became clear that the perfume in the glass animal-shaped bottles had been a big mistake. The stuff wasn't selling well at all. It seemed that humour and perfume just didn't go together. Maybe the lady customers saw its application as quite a serious business in the consideration of getting or keeping a man? Buttons, collar studs, combs, socks, reels of cotton, razor blades, elastic, though – all these mundane everyday items flew off the stall. The money mounted. I took money here, wrapped items there, traversing up and down the duckboards behind the stall like a ballet dancer.

Forward furtively came a shifty-eyed balding little man, sidling close. I had to listen keenly to make out his mumble. Sharp-eared Vince, though, caught the gist.

"Yeah, hang on a second," he said, pushing me aside. He stooped under the counter and arose clutching a small cream-painted tin, not dissimilar to the one I'd seen at The Prophet's. "Here you are. Rubbers. We sell them threepence cheaper than you get in the barber's or chemist's. Enjoy yourself!"

Red as a huntsman's coat, the man hurried down the length of the arch, jostling his way through milling bodies. Vince grinned. "Hear that, Stan? See the shy sex maniac doing a bunk? Reckon when he asks his old lady for anything more than a cuddle, she has to cup her ear'ole. Don't know whether he's feeling randy or only saying the hot water bottle's gorn stone cold."

The following week, Vince said to me, "This week I want you to have a go at the banter."

I gulped, looking embarrassed. "I don't really know what to say."

"If they're women, flatter 'em," he said. "Flatter 'em or flirt with 'em, whether they be nineteen or ninety. They all like it. And if they're men, praise 'em. 'Wise choice, sir. Those shirt studs are strong, made to last.' Praise the products, praise the customer."

Armed with this advice, I gave it a go. "Well, well, lady, nice bottle of perfume you've got there. Have a sniff. Reckon your old man will think you're the Queen of Sheba if you put that on when you get home!" The woman was of grandma age. She looked at me suspiciously and moved on.

"Not a bad try," said Vince, "but you've got to sound more convincing. Speak up. Have another go!"

So, I did. "Looking at those razor blades, are you, sir? Good choice. Nice and sharp. Made to last. Lots of shaves out of them, sir!"

"Not bad," said Vince. "At least you spoke up. Look, here's a young woman, not bad looking. Go on, flatter her!"

She was looking at the lipsticks. "Now, then, young, err, young lady," I stammered. "Looking at the lipsticks, are we? Reckon a lady with a lovely shade of blonde hair like yours would suit that pale pink."

She looked up amused. "And who let you out of your cot this morning?" she asked.

Vince gave me a dig in the ribs. "Keep going," he urged.

"Err, err, no-one. But me girlfriend kicked me out of bed!" I could hardly believe my temerity.

The girl laughed. But she bought the lipstick.

Vince was pleased. "That's more like it. Keep it up."

The following week, I was back on the stall with Vince, and we were unloading our boxes once again. One of them contained a new consignment, a load of artificial silk scarves.

"Prefer the real thing myself," Vince sniffed as we unpacked them. "Nothing like the feel of real silk, and these are nothing like the feel of real silk."

I looked at the scarves. They were in unappealing colours, either dun and dowdy greenish browns or dull navy blues.

Vince saw my look of disappointment. "Well, I got 'em cheap. Fell off the back of a lorry."

As we continued unpacking, he suddenly said, slyly, "Listen. I've got other places I want to be. I reckon you know enough now to run the stall by yourself. Keep up the spiel. I'll be back about five o'clock to lock up." And he sloped off.

And so I was left to run the stall on just my second day in the job.

Left to my own devices, I was surprised at just how deft and efficient I was. Even my embarrassment at having to reach under the counter to extract the cream tin wore off as I got used to it.

I still couldn't shift the scent in the amusing glass animal-shapes, though. The bottles continued to languish on the counter, just as they had the week before. Wondering why they were of such little interest, I thought I'd get the opinion of the women refusing to buy them. "What's wrong with them?" I asked a pleasant-looking woman who had just bought a reel of cotton.

"Well, we're women, son, not little girls. If my old man saw that on my dressing table, he'd reckon I'd gone soft. I like to see scent in something more sophisticated, like the bottles you see in the chemist."

It was a pity about the scent, I thought. Vince had bought a lot of the stuff, and if he ended up losing money on it, he might have to let me go. So, I thought, I had to find a way of selling it.

The scent itself wasn't too bad. Some of it smelt a bit like my mum's *4711*. The scent in the glass teddy bear was rich and spicy, like sandalwood. It was a shame that women weren't even bothering to unscrew the tops to sniff it. Those dreary scarves were a dead loss, too. They may have been cheap for Vince to buy, but their dull colours were not attracting the punters.

It was then that I got the idea.

I unscrewed the bottle of teddy bear scent and poured its woody aroma all over a brown scarf. Then I whirled the scarf round my head, dispersing its perfume generously into the air.

"Cor, what's that smell?" said an urchin, sniffing noisily, and inadvertently became my accomplice.

People began to take notice. "Mmm, nice smell. What's it called?" someone asked.

"*Sultry Sandalwood*!" I invented, spur of the moment. "All the way from Paris. Lovely aroma, lady." I handed over the scarf. "Here, lady, sniff that!"

The bottles began to sell. I poured the eau de cologne stuff over a blue scarf. "Here you are, ladies. *Memories at Midnight*. That's what this one's called."

Vince came back at five to find me in action, handing round scarves to sniff, selling bottle after bottle. He was pleased. "Thought I'd never see the day those bottles'd sell," he said.

So, takings were up, not down. I kept my job, and very soon I had amassed the fifty bob I needed. 'I'm off to get my suit now,' I thought gleefully. 'Stan Drewitt, prepare to grovel!'

Chapter 19

Things Get Serious

I strutted down Bridge Avenue with my £2 10s burning a hole in my pocket. I was quite literally rubbing my hands together with glee. I could not wait to reach the fifty bob tailors. I would make Stan Drewitt sweat. As I strutted, I looked ahead to our conversation... "Have you got a pale grey with a Saxe blue stripe? No. Close, but not quite the shade I was looking for. Material's quite thin, too. What about a pearl grey with a harebell blue stripe? Could you show me a swatch like that?" In my imagination, I could see him bringing me swatch after swatch of material for my approval, his teeth gritted, as he was forced to be polite in front of his superior.

As I entered the door, I breathed in the faint pleasant smell of cloth, and looked towards the long shiny oak counter. No Stan Drewitt. Just the smart proprietor preparing to ask, "May I help you, sir?"

"Is ... is ... Stan Drewitt here, please, sir?" Why did I sound so apologetic?

"No, he left for another job."

"Where?" This sounded a bit unnecessary.

"Kensington."

"Kensington!"

"Yes. Now, may I help you, sir?" This was said with carefully suppressed exasperation.

"Thank you, but I, err, I, err, had a message for him, and..." I backed out slowly, like a courtier backing away from an audience with a monarch.

Thwarted! Kensington!? I could hardly afford a suit from a shop in Kensington!

Dejectedly I trailed back home, and, on answering the door, mum said, "Well, did you get yourself a suit?"

"No, mum. Had second thoughts. Don't really need a suit. Reckon I could go for job interviews wearing my school uniform."

Stan Drewitt was no longer a problem for me. I didn't see much of him at all after that. It was rumoured that he was spending a lot of time up the West End. He'd met this aristocratic girl in a night club. She would toy with him for a while, amusing herself until she was ready to marry someone of her own class with the same cut glass accent as herself. Drewitt might have had the good looks to get himself a job in Kensington and a posh bird up West, but he would need to work on his vowel sounds if he wanted to up his game with girls like her.

Well on my way to being fifteen now, I would soon have to be thinking about getting a job. I was doing reasonably well at school, so I expected to get a good report and the office job so desired for me by mum.

I finally left school, having been presented with a loathsome book on Prizegiving Day, awarded for 'perseverance and good behaviour'. It was a book I thumbed through but would never read. It was called *Stoic*, and was all about a halo-deserving boy. He seized runaway horses, saving curly-haired little children from being trampled to death. He gave his last pennies to the poor. He helped little old ladies home with their groceries. How I hated the do-gooding little creep. The only thing I admired about the book was the ornate label on the flyleaf, a curving design of acanthus leaves in blue and red, tipped with gold. Mum admired it, of course, as did dad. Proud they were of a lad who had done so well at school, fulfilled all their hopes, got a good report. Now it was time for the serious business, though – I had to find myself a job.

The Central Schools Bureau in the City, near Snow Hill, was the place boys like myself went for job introductions. It was like a high-class labour exchange. I obtained my little green card, and was sent along to a Dickensian dungeon that was supposed to be a shipping office, but seemed more like a den of drudgery.

On entering, I thought I had entered a time warp. Clerks perched on stools, hunched over ledgers and bills, peering at long columns of spidery, ink-written figures. A Bob Cratchit-type figure, not much older than myself, jerked his head in the direction of the manager's office in response to my polite request of where to go for my interview.

Up to the glass-windowed cubicle I went, like I was approaching the admiral on the bridge of a ship. The manager was wearing pinstripes and a black high buttoned coat. Unsmiling, he had a face like a testy magistrate who had gone without his breakfast to get to court. He looked down at the card, up at me, and down at the card again. With a tone of annoyance in his voice, he said, wearily, "Have you had any clerical experience?"

"No, sir, I'm afraid not as yet."

"Hmph! Are you any good at figures?"

But the depressing atmosphere of the soul-destroying place was beginning to impinge on me. I made up my mind. "No!" I said. "Terrible. I wouldn't work here for a gold lollipop if I was down to my last ha'penny! What? Sit tight-arsed on one of those stools all day and add up millions and millions of figures for twenty-two and six a week? Never! My first sight of a shipping office and my last. Ta-Ta! This is me steaming out of here!"

Next, I got an interview for an office junior position at a solicitor's joint, way down old London's Cheapside, off the beaten track, down an alleyway, dozens of stairs past landings where more law firms were devilling away delaying cases getting to court until they'd found out just how much the client was worth. Dad said that's how they worked, and dad knew everything.

While I sat on a chair waiting to be summoned, I learned about the job from a senior junior clerk: lots of filing would be involved, and I'd be expected to make the tea. That put me off a bit, but I didn't mind too much. What really got up my nose was the delay of the start of the interview itself.

When I was called into the interview room, the junior solicitor nearly had his eyeballs touching a thick wad of papers stapled together. He just went on studying them, turning over page after page, then another, then another. He continued reading, silently ignoring me completely.

I began to feel warm, sitting there like a piece of shit not fit to be seen or spoken to. Warm, then hot about the collar. I became aware of my hands bunching into fists, my knees pressing in, and my toes impatiently tapping the faded but good quality carpet. I felt like a kettle about to blow steam. 'This geezer had better attend to me quick,' I thought. 'How much longer is he going to keep on reading, the rude-mannered arsehole?' The well-tended hand with a gold signet ring on its little finger turned over yet another typed page.

"Interesting, is it?" I finally enquired.

"I beg your pardon?"

"Beg? I'd rather beg or sell matches than work for you! Where I come from, we don't treat other people as though they were a nasty smell under the nose. Think you're so sophisticated, and you've got the manners of the gutter!" I headed for the door.

"I shall report you to the bureau, you ... you oaf!"

"Do that! I feel sorry for any young bloke you do eventually take on! Treat people like that, and one day you might get your cup of tea thrown all over your snotnose face!"

It pleased me leaving like that. No, I wasn't going to have a life of toadying and scraping to some despising boss-man. 'Here's your tea, sir, lick your boots, sir, may I dust your armpits, sir.' I skipped out into the street and jumped up and down the kerb like Gene Kelly in *Singin' in the Rain.*

"You mad, son?" a sweeper in front of a cart asked.

"Not mad, mate, just free. I'm going to live, I am. Not having my soul crushed by the bastards in that miserable dungeon. Don't know how I'm going to earn a crust, but it's not going to be in an office. Beg, borrow or steal, I'm going to be happy." That was my resolve.

When was I happiest? Working for Vince. I enjoyed the freedom of the banter with the customers, and seeing all the different tat acquired by Vince week by week. I liked the novelties: the plastic birds you filled with water and then blew through to make a tweeting noise; the coloured combs on cards; the smell of lavender brilliantine. It was lively, bustling, it made me feel good. Ten shillings a day, six days a week, and that would bring me in three whole pounds. As a junior clerk, I would be lucky to get twenty-five shillings a week!

Reaching Angel Walk, I thought to myself that I didn't need the Central Schools Bureau. I didn't need a job in an office. I remembered that I had a way of making people buy things, a talent for getting rid of stuff that stuck on the stall, like the novelty bottles of scent. I was an asset to Vince, and he knew it. So, rather than go straight home, I headed for Vince's.

Louise opened the door to my bold knock.

"Vince, Stan Tinsley here to see you."

"Why is he here? Ain't Saturday."

"Dunno."

He came to the door.

"Vince, err, Mr. Collins. I've got an idea. I've left school now, and I could work for you full time, and…"

But I was interrupted. "Work for me full time? Couldn't afford that, son. Saturday is my busiest day, and I don't need any help during the week. Sorry. See you Saturday as usual, or do you have to work half-day Saturdays now you've left school?"

"No, Mr. Collins. I haven't got a job yet. Thank you." Dejectedly, I turned and trailed back down the path, a quote from my schoolwork drifting into my head: 'Shades of the prison house begin to close upon the growing boy.'

Drudgery loomed, then. The dull, dim drudgery of an office job.

Chapter 20

In Disgrace

You've got a lot to learn, son," Dad said gravely, after I had told him about the altercation with the sneering young solicitor at the interview. "You can't afford to intimidate stuck up snobs like him."

"But, dad, what about that woman on the horse, the one you told off when…"

"That's different. She had no power over me. I'll probably never see her again in my life. But if you get a bad report with the Bureau, he could spoil things for you, make it difficult to get a job."

"Your father's right, Stanley," said mum, standing by his chair, backing him up. "You should have kept your lip buttoned, should have swallowed your pride."

I felt warmth rising up in me, hot indignation. "I went along to that interview ready to be pleasant. I worked hard at school and got good reports. Then I was treated like a piece of shit, and…"

"You can't buck the system," interrupted dad. "I know it's unfair, but you can't fight the establishment."

"You need to get a job, young man," said mum solemnly. "Your father bought the school uniform, gave you extra for bus fares."

"And I'm expected to be bloody grateful," I sneered, and instantly regretted my tone.

"Don't speak to your mother like that!" dad exploded. "Where's all that fine schooling gone? The manners we taught you? A year back, I thought you were coming on nicely. Now it seems I might be getting a corner boy for a son!"

"I'm going up to my room!" I announced, before the hot tears threatened to spill down my cheeks. It was so unfair. In all good faith I had gone to that interview, in all good faith!

It was dad's diminutive friend Perce who eventually got me a job. It's not what you know, it's who you know, as the old saying goes, and Perce knew a man who knew a man...

The job was in an insurance office and paid twenty-five shillings a week for a five-and-a-half-day week. Regrettably, I had to give up the Saturday job with Vince. The only thing I had to look forward to now was the Sunday walk with dad, but if it rained Sundays were bleak indeed. The bells of St. Paul's church would toll persistently, of course, calling the faithful to worship. They seemed to be saying:

> *Ding dong*
> *You are so wrong*
> *Ding dong*
> *Come along, come along*

But we weren't church goers. Dad said his prayers every night, but he had no time for organised religion. "Sanctimonious lot, walking to church looking miserable as sin. Vicar going on and on and on. If you want to talk to the Lord, why do you need church? Reckon He's going to listen to you anyway without their interference."

Mum had gone to church in her youth, and persuaded me to go once, just once. I had felt uncomfortable kneeling on the hard tapestry hassocks, intoning the depressing chant, 'We have erred and strayed from thy ways like lost sheep.' I had resented the words 'miserable offenders'. I was no saint, but I did not regard myself as a miserable offender.

So, on rainy Sundays, I read in my room and tried to ignore the intrusive sound of those bells.

Work on weekdays and half-day Saturday was all right. Not exciting like the market stall, but tolerable, and it paid twenty-five shillings a week, a *tosheroon* more than the job I may have got in the solicitor's office, had I been prepared to be servile. A *tosheroon* was two and sixpence, and could buy you a good night out with a girl in Hammersmith, back then. Pictures, café, sweets, bus fares. I had the money for it now. The only thing I needed was a girl. I had been introduced to flirting by Vince, but it wasn't the same as actually getting a girlfriend. The customers came and went, and some were old enough to be my grandmother.

I could afford to buy myself some decent clothes. I got a nice grey suit with a cream stripe from the fifty bob tailors, and a cream shirt in artificial silk from Orton's. My pride and joy, though, was my silk kipper tie, real silk, with three girls' heads pictured on it, a blonde, a brunette and a redhead. It had cost me a fortune, ten and six, and mum loathed it.

"What will people think with you walking along the street wearing that awful vulgar thing! Why you couldn't get yourself a nice tasteful tie like the kind of ties that Mr. Andrews wears, I really don't know." Mr. Andrews was a scoutmaster who lived a few doors down from us. He had a well-paid job working for the railway, some sort of office job, and was the sort of person mum wanted me to look up to as a role model. He was ultra-polite. He had a smartly-dressed wife, and a little baby who always seemed to break into tears and howls as I walked past its over-large pram parked outside their front door. Out in all weathers, was the poor little mite. Andrews was of an intrepid frame of mind, and believed in fitness and fresh air. I loathed him. Mum had tried to get me to join the cubs once, but I had adamantly refused, saying that sporty pursuits and earning badges was not for me. With a sigh, she had given up.

I had the suit, I had the money, but I did not have the girl. Where could I meet a girl? The girls along my road were all going steady now, had been working for over two years. There was only Olivia who was single, and I knew very well that Olivia, a very pretty Italian girl, was out of my league.

The 'eye-ties', as they were called in those days, were highly respected by dad. "Good business people, the eye-ties," he would say.

"Nice clean cafés; work hard; pleasant."

Olivia's family lived in a big house which they had all to themselves, even the basement, and owned a café in the Broadway. That was where Olivia worked. She had glossy dark hair which she coiled on top of her head, and she was always smartly dressed, with a penchant for flowery voile dresses and matching Cuban heeled shoes.

"Buongiorno!" I had called out cheekily on passing her.

"Good morning," she had politely replied.

Nothing doing with Olivia. If I wanted to find a girlfriend, I would have to get out and about.

On my free Saturday afternoons, I resolved to go out for a long walk in the direction of Castelnau on my way to Barnes Common. Striding towards Hammersmith Bridge, I had the exhilarating experience of standing high above a string of barges, trailing chicks after a mother duck tug, giving me the sensation of floating out weightless and wafting with them. With few people about (not that I would have cared anyway), I jumped on to a plank seat as a big Foden steam wagon chuffed, road-bound locomotive-like, over the reverberating suspension bridge. It was great to enjoy the movement of the seat, springing shakily.

Along Castelnau and by the tall railings trapping the still silver waters of the timelessly becalmed reservoir. Over the far side of the road trundled, clop and clatter, a slow-moving coal cart, chalk on rod-tied card saying its load was 'Derby Brights', there in those slumpy sacks. With a bobbing fringe over its wide forehead, a shaggy white horse ploddingly drew on the cart, its horny hooves sprouted with tufts of hair the shade of dead grass. At the swaying metal back step lower down, a small boy crouched, stealing a ride. I smiled, remembering how I had done the very same thing some years ago. I was almost an adult now, but still felt like a boy sometimes. Passing the stone eagles guarding the big house where G.H. Chirgwin, 'The White-Eyed Kaffir' of music hall fame, used to live, I felt loneliness dropping down on me in a sudden unexpected sadness.

In the select quietude of almost village-like Barnes High Street, I visited the fruiterers and bought a pound of cool redskin apples. While the shop man dug for change in the till, I palmed a fat and velvety peach. Its oozy, syrupy juice sweet-wet my sampling, munching mouth, as I went all round the back streets to approach the extensive Common's embankment-boundaried and tree-bordered cricket field. Restful and really relaxing it was, just sitting there biting into crispy red apples while watching the raised vista of green, snaking trains sliding by. All by herself, lonely at a carriage window, sat a woman studiously reading a book, then she stared out vacantly, surely not seeing me spit out a pip.

Until I turned my head at the animal's pah-pah-panting, I wasn't aware of a girl with a dog. He was a tan retriever with a lengthy wet tongue, York ham pink, full of frothy foam slaver, but with friendly brown eyes. Smiling, I back-rubbed the calm cherry hog all over down to its flick-flick tail, patted its silky head, gently rubbed its right ear, then its left. Out of the corner of my shrewdly observing eye, I saw the onset of approval over my actions: the girl's lightly rose-tinted lips forming a very nice curve of a smile.

"Sandy, behave! You will muss the gentleman's suit," she said.

"It's all right."

She sat down fluidly, smoothing her skirt. Her hair was shiny, her skin a delicate porcelain, unpowdered. Sea blue eyes, a trusting innocence. A suit, she had on, made of some countrified cloth, a mixture of leaf green and autumn brown.

"A pleasant day," she remarked.

"A pleasant day for what?" I said, sounding far too suggestive.

"For a leisurely stroll and a run with Sandy." She sounded like a high school girl with the airy nonchalance of the privileged. "Setting out from home, one never knows what will happen, does one? I find that through Sandy I get into conversation with the most interesting people."

"Oh," I said, sliding along the seat to get nearer. "I'm not just interesting; I'm double fascinating. When you get to know me, that is. What's your name? Guinevere? Sitting all Princess Charming like that."

She tittered almost childishly, and fluttered her hand, bird-like.

"You are funny. Frances, you may call me, because I do so detest people abbreviating it to Frankie, as though I were a boy. You, now, look to me like a George ready to take on a dragon."

"It's Nigel Fanshawe."

"Nigel Fanshawe! That is nice. Quite novelettish. Nigel

Fanshawe. Fancy that."

Casually, deceptively slowly, I crawled a long arm along the top, headrest slat of the seat, brushing the material clinging to her slender shoulders.

The amiable dog was snuffling patiently among the short grasses and weeds growing round the seat. "Sit!" Frances commanded, and though her voice piped musically high, it also rang with a peal of authority.

"I am," I said.

"You are what?"

"Sitting. It sounded as if you were ordering me about like a cheeky young puppy."

"Oh, you are an ass. I don't know what to make of you. I don't believe you are called Nigel Fanshawe, either. I believe you made that up." She shifted in her seat, revealing more of her silkily-stockinged legs.

"Nice pair of legs you've got there, Frances. Nice figure, too, in that suit."

She winced at the familiarity, and blushed a convolvulus pink. "Now you are being rather too personal."

"Personal? Can't you take a compliment? I thought girls liked a bit of flattery." I knew as soon as it came out how clumsy that sounded, but, at sixteen years old, I still had a lot to learn about girls. Annie was a distant memory now. Boys who had left school at fourteen were so much more streetwise than I was. One was even a father at seventeen, and after his hasty marriage had gone to live in scruffy Cardross Street, and even that was in lodgings.

"Flattery! Well, really! There aren't many girls about here of the sort you are plainly used to. Good afternoon. Come along, Sandy!"

I sat there with a silly grin on my face, feeling foolish and embarrassed.

I was aware of a dark-suited youth heading in my direction, disengaging himself from the tree he had been leaning against. I had been vaguely aware of his presence, but had not really taken much notice of him. Now he approached me and said, "Wotcher, mate! That was a right fox's pass you made with that pretty bird. Scared her off something rotten."

The newcomer flung himself down on the seat, making it rock. His carroty hair was up-brushed, making him appear startled, and his heart-shaped face was deceptively angelic and dimpled of cheek.

"Mind your own!" I retorted. "Hoppit! I don't like people stagging on what I'm up to!"

"Don't be like that. I wasn't purposely spying." Undaunted, my companion settled himself comfortably, crossing one pinstriped leg over the other to reveal nattily-clocked white on black socks. "All I was wondering was where your technique went wrong. That toffee-nosed tart is always proudly parading over here, exercising the dog. One or two optimistic yobs have tried to chat her up, but to my knowledge she's cocked a deaf 'un to every slick spiel. Pretty damn well you did in getting her to speak at all."

"That true? That I'm the first to get her chatting?" I queried eagerly.

"Too right, but girls like that really only take boys seriously who have been introduced to them at parties and tennis clubs. Sons of their daddy's friends. If you want to get anywhere with girls, you'll have to join the Monkey Parade."

I knew all about the Monkey Parade. On a Saturday night, boys and girls, some as young as fourteen, dressed in their best clothes and walked in pairs with friends of the same sex, hoping to be picked up, the girls giving coy glances in the direction of boys they fancied, waiting for a chat up line.

"What's your name, anyway?" I asked, eyeing him up suspiciously.

"Phil. Phillip Walsh. Now, don't laugh, but I could do with a mate. Trouble is, see, the girls go around with a mate, and they like to start off with a foursome. Then you all walk round for a while, and then suggest the pictures or the amusement arcade. Got to be prepared to spend a bit of money on them."

"I know the drill. Where d'you live, Phil?"

"East Acton. On the Flower Estate."

"I know it. Where the streets are named after begonias and suchlike. You working?"

"Between jobs. I start in a gents' outfitting shop less than three weeks from now. Learning to work my way up to first salesman."

"Hmm. So you'll have a half-day off in the week, like I have?"

"How's that? Do you go in for a spot of slavery, too?"

"Insurance office. Boring, but not too bad. Me, I'd rather be a spieler on a big market stall, flogging bits and bobs and novelties, knickknacks of all sorts."

"You haven't told me your name yet," said Phil.

"Stan. Stan Tinsley from the 'Smith. Well, if we're going to join the Monkey Parade, where you want to meet?"

"What about outside Hammersmith Woolworth's, six o'clock?"

"Suits me."

In a way I had come of age. I was about to join the Monkey Parade.

Chapter 21

Phyllis and Phoebe

Saturday evening, six o'clock.

I was early, so I paused at the frontage of Hammersmith Palace of Varieties, entering a few feet inside the foyer to study a framed photograph of Talbot O'Farrell, the faux-Irish wit of the immaculate grey suiting and tall silk hat, whose affected rich brogue somehow enhanced the slyness of his humour. A few seconds wasted, I crossed over to stand outside Woolworth's to wait impatiently for Phil.

Phil was on time. He swaggered up to the entrance, weak sunlight falling on his copper knob hair. A palmful of brilliantine had darkened it, making it the colour of an Irish setter's pelt, wet from a River Thames dip.

I was new to this game, so Phil was the leader, rather as Vince had been my mentor in the market job. We turned with a swishy little swerve into the King Street. Phil gave me a nudge. "Watch out for two good lookers. We don't want one of us being envious and resenting the one who got the best looking."

Pairs of girls were ambling along the street, all dressed in their best. What a profusion of different blouses! There were blouses fancy and frilly, white silk sheer blouses with drawstrings at the hem, blouses floral in riots of peonies, pansies and poppies, chiffon blouses with intricate embroidery, some beautifully worked in *broderie anglaise*, all displayed for our approval.

"What sort of girls do you like, Stan?" asked Phil.

"Ones with not too much make up, and hair looking natural. Can't stand some of these daft fashions where they make kiss curls and stick them to their cheeks with soap, or with a fringe so long you wonder how they can see."

There was such a variation of hair styles. Most went in for short styles, bobs, page boys, little piles of curls on the crown. Girls with dark hair tended to go for a Dolores del Rio look, smoothing down their hair with olive oil. These would-be Latins were probably from Lisgar Terrace or Peabody Buildings, and had never been within miles of a sunlit piazza, chewing gum in their teeth rather than a rose.

Not easy finding girls with nicely natural hair. Some had dyed it yellow-blonde with peroxide in an attempt to look like Jean Harlow. Some had dyed one side of their hair blonde and left the other side their natural colour, or had one peroxide lock lying like a dead thing in the centre of different coloured hair.

We passed by Payne's the butchers, where bright red saveloys, faggots, and ochre-coloured pease pudding had been put out in trays on a bench. "Look at the steam! Just been put out. The saveloys will bite into red hot."

"Never mind the saveloys! There's two smashers coming this way," Phil urged. "Let them pass and cop us smiling side on, then we'll fall in behind and chat."

This we did, and, in the manner of the day, employed the expected ridiculously banal icebreaker dialogue.

"I'm very partial to blondes," began Phil, "particularly when their hair is as shiny as that."

I caught on. "I prefer redheads, myself. Did you ever see such a smashing auburn shade?"

Frankly, for a visitor from another planet it would have been most amusing to watch and marvel at this initial contact procedure. As was normal when hopefully spoken to, the girls put on speed of progress in going hell for leather for nowhere. And all along the considerably populated Monkey Parade, other boys and girls were carrying on as we were, the boys moving in for the persuasive preliminary speech, then everyone in the close quartet quickening pace to little less than a run. In places, couples were peeling off from the colourful parade, heading for the back seat of the pictures, or hurrying happily on to the Cosy Corner Café for cod, chips and cracklings, or maybe preferring the amusement arcade.

Phil gave me a broad wink. "I wonder if these two have got names?"

My hoped-for redhead turned her head a few degrees: slow, studied sly. She batted her lashes prettily and looked demurely away.

"I don't know your name, love," persisted Phil, targeting the blonde. "Wonder what it begins with."

"It begins with 'P'," said the blonde.

174

"Penelope?"

"Nothing like."

"Patricia, then?"

"Not that either."

"Let's see... Petunia? Philomena? Poppy? Pam?"

"What does your name begin with?" I cautiously asked the redhead.

"Same as hers. 'P'. I'm Phyllis and she's Phoebe."

Phyllis was clearly tired of the initial chat. She wanted to cut to the chase and get in on some entertainment. We were expected to pay, of course.

Phoebe butted in. "Already seen the Paul Muni film this week. Let's go to the amusement arcade and then for a drink."

"Suits me. Right, we'll go." It was taken for granted by the dominant Phil that I would agree.

We passed by the snake swimming tanks of the eel and pie shop, swivelled, and waited for the Broadway traffic to stop. A gap in the stream, we ran across to enter the alley between the shops which led to the amusement arcade. The grumble-rumble of the dodgem cars reached us, escaping whenever anyone left through the door far ahead.

Phil pushed through the panelled swing door and we entered the brightly-lit fug beyond. The arcade was a clicking, pinging, whirring, light-flickering realm. A long, pin-tabled aisle stretched away to the right of the ring-stepped arena of the dodgem cars. These bright-enamelled, bug-like pods of slow bumpy progress fizzed out winking blue sparks from their current-carrying back-poles. They were first up for entertainment, naturally, and we enjoyed a bumping and shrieking ten minutes on them, with Phyllis and Phoebe clinging on to our arms.

Next was the steel crane grab. We all looked at the prizes trapped behind glass beneath the silvery closed claws of the miniature crane: packets of Player's, their shiny cellophane clutch-resistant; lighters, their width wider than the meagre yawn opening of the grab; combs of good length, which held for a moment, then slipped and dropped.

Under the experienced tutelage of Phil, there were more nights out on the Monkey Parade. Some girls were shy, reserved: others bolder. If the hippies think they invented the permissive society in the sixties, they were thirty years too late. The casual approach to sexual encounters was alive and well and prevalent in 1930s London. I had taken on board what The Prophet had taught me, and his warnings made sense. Before the invention of the pill, it was the man's responsibility to 'take care' of his girlfriend, and the good old reliable French letter prevented many an unwanted 'little stranger'.

How could I have known, a few months into my sixteenth birthday, what lay ahead? I remember the day well: September 3rd, 1939. It was a Sunday, and we were listening to the wireless. Alvar Liddell, the radio newscaster, told everyone to stand by for an important announcement. At a few minutes past eleven came the speech from Neville Chamberlain, the Prime Minister, which ended with the life-changing words...

"This morning, the British ambassador in Berlin handed the German government a final note stating that unless we heard from them by eleven o'clock that they were prepared at once to withdraw their troops from Poland, a state of war would exist between us. I have to tell you now that no such undertaking has been received, and that consequently this country is at war with Germany."

Afterword

by Barbara Tinsley

This is where my father's manuscript ends, and two years later he was called up to serve in the army. He was assigned to the Durham Light Infantry and eventually sent to Egypt, but it was before that, while he was stationed at Brancepeth Castle near Durham, that he first saw my mother. Travelling back to barracks on the bus one evening, he saw her, then fifteen, walking along Crook High Street. She took his fancy, and he got off the bus and chatted her up. Mum, a miner's daughter from Willington, was swayed by his Cockney charm. They married, moved to London after the war, and lived in 29 Angel with my Grandma and Grandad. I arrived on the 14th of August 1947.

How lucky was I to have spent my childhood in Angel Walk! I inherited Grandma and Grandad's bedroom after they retired to Suffolk when I was about four. So much of what dad wrote about in his manuscript about that room is familiar to me from my time occupying it. The marble washstand with the china jug and bowl patterned with blue Arabs and camels; the big bed with the brass knobs; the huge double-doored wardrobe – all these furnished my bedroom. By the side of the iron fireplace was a cupboard lined with blue pomegranate wallpaper. Above the fireplace was a huge mirror with small side shelves. And to the left of the window was an alcove in which I kept my sadly unappreciated doll's house, which dad had made.

Fortunately for me, the large patch of waste ground 'over the wall' had still not been developed by the time I lived in the house. In fact, there was even more to it, as the builder's yard which had occupied part of it in dad's day was now gone. There it was, my own private patch of countryside, brimming with wild flowers, buddleia shrubs and blackberry bushes. One old buddleia had such gnarled and twisted branches they had formed a kind of wicker cage, and I would crawl inside and read for hours: *Billy Bunter*, *Just William*, and every Enid Blyton book ever written. I couldn't stand *Swallows and Amazons*, though, or *Winnie the Pooh*; the children in those stories always seemed to me to be way too priggish. Like his mother before him, dad taught me to read before I went to school, so I was an avid reader back then. But later, training to be a teacher and having to learn boring facts to pass exams rather killed my life as a bookworm.

There were trees to climb, over the wall. There was a lilac bush from which to gather blooms. But, most importantly of all, there was The Forbidden Garden. Separating this mysterious domain from my patch was the garden of an inhabited house. I could glimpse the trees and shrubs of the secret territory from a distance, but knew that they belonged to The Derelict House. Of this I was afraid, just as my father had been all those years before. Inevitably, one day I did climb the wall of the inhabited house's garden, then ran across their lawn and grasped the top of the opposite wall, swung up and over, and dropped with trepidation into the lost world beyond. There, exactly as dad describes it from his own memories, was the gazebo. Its wooden slats had flaking blue paint, and there was no door, just an aperture through which I glimpsed those photographs of sepia-tinted ladies in the costumes of principal boys. As my father describes, these pictures were still in their intact glass-fronted frames. There was a smell of decay and rotten wood. The place looked like it was stuck in a time warp. Who had lived there? I was conscious that at the bottom of the long and overgrown garden stood the old house. In front of the gazebo was a blackcurrant bush on which there were luscious fruits which I quickly ate. I did not see the raspberry bushes dad had described, perhaps because they weren't as yet bearing fruit. I did not stay long. The place had a feeling of unseen eyes, and I was glad to escape and get back home. I cannot remember visiting it more than once. Dad had never mentioned it to me. Maybe he was afraid for me to go there, a small girl on her own in such a lonely place. Who knows who might have been there?

Dad was such an interesting playmate. Like his father, he was an improviser of games. He would sometimes suddenly call, "Rowing boats!" and, sole to sole, we would sit on the floor and pull each other over and back, just as grandad had done with his game of Oxford and Cambridge. Dad continued the tradition of homemade wine; I was assigned to gather dandelions, of which there were plenty, and the ensuing wine was like a mellow whisky. He also made 'gold dust' out of crushed Marie biscuits, cocoa powder and sugar, but I did not care much for that. One of my favourite games was 'archaeologists'. This consisted of going out into the garden and digging. We found much iridescent glass from old bottles and bits of broken china. I used to lay it all out on a marble slab, which had once been the top of the scullery table, and now resided beside the wall in the garden.

Dad had inherited a love of the country, and we would go out on the Green Line bus, armed with one of mum's blackberry pies, if the old blackberry bush at the bottom of our garden was still flourishing. Mum, like grandma before her, often struggled over stiles and was afraid of cows, so, after a few outings, gracefully withdrew to leave future adventures to dad and myself. It was gentle, easy walking country, with sunken tracks arched over with graceful beech trees, and fields full of flowers; scabious, scarlet pimpernel, cornflowers and poppies. How people can enjoy punishing walks up unforgiving barren hills in flowerless landscapes, I really do not know.

Dad was full of humour. For instance, dinner might bring forth an old joke...

"How long's dinner going to be, mum?"

"Six inches – it's a sausage."

Alternatively, he might recite, "The boy stood on the burning deck, with half a sausage round his neck."

This noble boy, who scrupulously maintained his post on the burning deck when all but he had fled, was, of course, the subject of much ridicule. Up would jump dad, assuming a striking pose, to declare:

The boy stood on the burning deck,
His feet were covered in blisters,
His trousers had all burnt away
So he had to borrow his sister's.

Or,

The boy stood on the burning deck,
When all but he had fled.
Why!?

There was much laughter in our house and I can never remember being bored. Like grandma's dreams of an office job for dad, however, dad had aspirations for me. He wanted me to be a teacher, an ambition I eventually achieved. In later years, bogged down with paperwork and the endless marking, marking, marking of books, I would look back to my old Saturday job in Sloane Square Woolworth's and say, "If I had my life over again, I would have stayed in Woolworth's." Bored to distraction in his new job at Milburngate Post Office Savings Bank, dad would often say, "If only I could have taken over Vince's stall when he retired." History repeats itself.

As for the people in Angel Walk, old Mrs. Price was still there, a kindly lady now in her eighties who would often give me sweets. The Italian family, old and retired now, still inhabited the big house. But The Prophet, the Lavender Sisters and the odious Stan Drewitt were long gone.

Orton's, the elegant haberdasher's, was still there, with its glass-fronted, room-like windows. I remember that a set of handkerchiefs adorned with pictures of Mabel Lucie Attwell's chubby children had pride of place in one of the side windows, and the assistants still wore black dresses and sent tubes of money flying up to the cabined cashier. Did Joycie still work there? Had I unknowingly seen her as a middle-aged woman, her grotto days long gone? In my childhood, children seldom played in the street, and grottoes were a thing of the past. I had no idea of their existence until I read about them in my father's manuscript.

The lively bustle of old Cockney London seems to be a thing of the past. I see on Google Street View that Hammersmith Market is now a paved mall with the ubiquitous chain stores and cafés, Starbucks, for example. As a child, I remember the old costermongers there, their barrows covered with artificial grass calling out their wares: "Ripe and lovely peaches, ladies, ripe and lovely peaches"; and, at Christmas, "Lovely 'olly, all berry!"

Outside the butcher's, whole rabbits, their heads in small buckets to catch the blood, were on sale. Who would skin them now? Not me! Sheep's heads, pig's trotters, complete turkeys, still feathered, and with limp hanging necks: this was the kind of thing sold in old Hammersmith Market. The seafood stall had little china plates with whelks, cockles, and shrimps. When I bought a portion, I drenched them with vinegar and pepper and ate them with the cocktail stick provided.

Old Uncle Jack sometimes visited us. He had a strange expression for surprise and admiration: "Well strike me pink!"

Uncle Ned, last of the Edwardians, always smart with grey suit, watch chain and waxed moustache, used to come to see us, too, when I was very young. I didn't like him, though, because he would throw me up in the air and catch me and kiss me, which I detested. Then, one day, I said stoutly, "I don't like you!" which was very rude of me and which mortified my poor mother, who blustered and flustered and said with a red face, "Heh, heh, she says that to everybody!" Uncle Ned never came again.

I had a unique and interesting childhood, thanks to life in good old Angel Walk, and I enjoyed the legacy handed down to me by my grandparents. I often wonder what my life would have been had the old house not been under threat of demolition, causing dad to leave London. Would I have stayed at Woolworth's? If so, I would not have met the good and treasured friends I have now. Perhaps it was all for the best, then.

But who knows?